Jennifer
May God bless
you in the study
of His word!
You are God's
designing Woman!

Pam

MAKING DESIGNING WOMEN
OUT OF
DESPERATE HOUSEWIVES

Pam Sims

CROSSBOOKS
PUBLISHING

CrossBooks™
A Division of LifeWay
1663 Liberty Drive
Bloomington, IN 47403
www.crossbooks.com
Phone: 1-866-879-0502

First published by CrossBooks 10/19/2011

ISBN: 978-1-4627-0579-5 (sc)
ISBN: 978-1-4627-1018-8 (e)
ISBN: 978-1-4627-0580-1 (hc)
Library of Congress Control Number: 2011914691

Printed in the United States of America

This book is printed on acid-free paper.

The scriptures quoted are from the New American Standard Bible unless otherwise noted.

DEDICATION

This book is dedicated to my friend Sheryl Mulberry who spent hours upon hours editing this work and to the memory of her two sons, Keith and Jacob who lost their lives while she was working on this project. She is a dedicated wife and mother who exemplifies the women in this book.

CONTENTS

PREFACE

For the past several years God has been leading me on a journey. My life has taken some unexpected turns and bends along the way. Although I may not have chosen this path for my life, it is the life I have been given to live. The desire of my heart is for this work to express my heart and my passion for a loving and faithful Father in heaven who has brought me to this place. In my journey through life I have met many women who have, in one way or another, exemplified the *Proverbs 31* woman. Many great books have been written about this woman. I pray that you find that patterning your life after this woman is not an impossible task, and that these pages that will inspire you to do so.

While we may never possess all her qualities, we can learn from her how we ought to reflect those qualities as wives, mothers, sisters, daughters and friends. We can choose to live our life under the direction of a loving, merciful, heavenly father who will mold our character into His likeness. My heart's desire *is* that my family and friends will see these qualities in me. It is also my prayer that you find this book helpful in your own journey. It is a journey for life becoming such a woman, but one worth taking. We no longer need to be living as ***desperate housewives***. Each of us began our journey as daughters and granddaughters. Some are sisters, cousins, and nieces. Many of us have entered into another phase of our life as wives, mothers, aunts and even grandmothers. With each phase of our lives come new challenges to face. There will be new directions to take and mistakes to be made and learned from. Welcome, ladies, to discovering who God wants you to be! ***A woman by God's design.***

INTRODUCTION

Have you ever really wondered just who was this woman they called the Proverbs 31 woman. I know I have. I read commentaries about her, but they seemed to spend very little time on the verses. So why do we, (and I am assuming you, because you have the book,) want to know is she too perfect to be real. Let me let you in on a little secret before we begin reading. She is real. I want you to know just what I have discovered about her that maybe you did not know. I am not a theologian, so just relax; I don't talk in theological terms in this book. I hope I am very much like you.

The book is meant to encourage you. Nothing is impossible with God, right? Of course, you have heard that before, but there are just some things in life that *seem* impossible. The stories in this book are stories of women in the Bible, who have in one way or another, displayed in their lives some of the characteristics of the woman we read about in Proverbs 31, and some who have not.

Not all women in the Bible were good, but God used even some of those women to teach us something about Himself, His love, His character and even His judgment. We learn from our mistakes. We grow in grace when we acknowledge that He alone is God.

We will look at each verse in this passage, and it is my prayer that you will laugh with me, pray with me, grow with me. Because every time I read or reread a portion of this book I ask God to teach me something. I have read it out loud so that I will know the content of what is written.

Each chapter I pray will bring insight for you into the life, and into the heart of this amazing woman. Notice that she does not have a name, or a face. We think we know who she was because of the beginning verses in the chapter, but I think there is a reason that we aren't given her name. She is YOU. You are the woman by God's design. He created this woman in the same way He created you.

He gave you special gifts and abilities that no one else has. He equipped you with supernatural instincts, and abilities that will confound and surprise the world. You have a keen sense of fairness, a deep devoted love of family, you are a nurturer, a woman on a mission, and you are compassionate, tender and loving. You work tirelessly for the good of your family. You enjoy the small things. You care or you wouldn't have bought this book.

This book is not a substitute for the Holy Word of God; at the end of each chapter you will find challenging questions that will guide you into a deeper walk. You can choose to do those alone or with a friend.

Making Designing Women Out of Desperate Housewives is a book about all of us. Women. Young and old, single or married. We all need Jesus. That is why I am so glad that you have chosen to walk with me through this journey. I hate going it alone. You are special to God. He is so in love with you. His desire for you is that you become a desperate woman. Desperate for Him. Desperate for what He wants to give to you.

Now let's grab a cup of coffee (*I have always wanted to say that, but I prefer a Dr. Pepper*) and close off the world for a little while and learn what made this women so special that God would write about her in His word. You are so special to God; there is nothing He won't do for you and nothing He won't do in you, when you call on Him so, let's pray together as we begin.

Lord, I am so glad that you made us women. I know that You must love us very much because You have shown us through Your word just how much we mean to You. You are our Father, and because You love us, You want to teach us to become the best wives, mothers, sisters and friends that we can be.

You have given us Your Word as a light for our path. You show us our weakness and our need of a Savior. You bring victory into our lives over sin and death. You raise us up to walk when we cannot stand. You have made us in Your image, and we have your Holy Spirit as our guide. Thank you most of all for sending Your son, our Savior, to be the light in our dark world. We are desperate to become a pearl of great price and a woman by God's design. Amen.

Design #1
"DIAMONDS ANYONE?"

Proverbs 31:10 - **A good woman is hard to find
and worth far more than diamonds.**[1]

I have never really watched the show Desperate Housewives, but I like the title because it fits most women in our society today, not in the way you see us portrayed on the television show, but in a way that brings us to the point of our need. We are desperate for God's help in designing us to represent God's beauty in human flesh.

As little girls we all wanted to be Snow White or Cinderella, and some day grow up and marry Prince Charming. We wanted to be swept off our feet and taken to some castle where we we're pampered for the rest of our lives. However, when reality hit us, after the honeymoon, most of us were left with dirty diapers and dirty dishes at the end of the day. We certainly did not see ourselves as being worth more than diamonds. We found ourselves looking into the mirror and crying, "Mirror, mirror on the wall, who's the fairest of them all?" only to have the mirror shout back, "Well, honey, it isn't you." We, more often than not, see ourselves as rocks rather than diamonds.

Ladies, if you are to be considered a diamond then you must be the real deal. Today we have synthetic diamonds and other synthetic jewels

---

1   *THE MESSAGE* is quoted: "scripture taken from *THE MESSAGE.* Copyright © 1993, 1994, 1995,1996,2000,2001, 2002. Used by permission of NavPress Publishing Group."

that only a qualified jeweler can identify. He or she has been trained to recognize a fake diamond, and it would be very difficult to pass a synthetic diamond off as the real thing.

Many women out there are trying to pass themselves off as real diamonds, when in reality their lives are synthetic. Let me see if I can explain. All of my life I have been active in church. I know how to act the part of a churchwoman. I can pray out loud. I have served on committees, sung in the choir, played the piano, and taught Sunday School. For years, I was fooling everyone in church except for God about who I was. Outwardly, I practiced Christianity, but inwardly my life was synthetic. I looked the part, but I was not who I claimed to be. I had to **get real** with God. He knew who I was long before I would admit it to myself. Many of you who read this may have been living your life as a synthetic diamond just like I did. One of the greatest verses for me in all of scripture came when I finally realized that I needed to be obedient to God, and that my life was a work in progress. That verse was Philippians 1:6 "For I am confident of this very thing, that He who began a good work in you will perfect it until the day of Christ Jesus."[2] I came to be at peace with knowing that I could not ever be perfect, but that I could *strive* to be perfect. I would fail, but God would always be there to continue to work in me. God, who begins the work, will finish the job.

A woman who lacks noble character may be able to fool some of the people she is around, but eventually her true character is going to come out. Even if she can pull it off, God knows what she is really like. An excellent woman, a woman of noble character is worth her weight in gold. Proverbs 12:4 tells us: "An excellent wife is the crown of her husband, but she who shames him is as rottenness to his bones." [3]

We live in an age where women are not too concerned about what their husbands think of them. Many women view this as showing some kind of weakness. It is rather a sign of disrespect. We are encouraged to be independent, strong and self-reliant. We work outside the home, take care of the children, and do the laundry (*some of us, my husband does our laundry*). We cook, clean, take the kids to ball practice, and piano lessons, we are even the chairperson of the PTA. We need to be wearing a crown

2   The New American Standard Bible ©1960,1962,1968,1971,1972,1973,1975,1 977 by the Lockman Foundation. Used by permission.
3   The New American Standard Bible.

on our heads and a super hero outfit *(one that makes us look like Wonder Woman)*, singing, "I am woman, hear me roar! So buddy don't push your luck or your will find yourself out on your ear, because I don't need you."

This is certainly not a picture of the excellent woman. We are to act in such a way as to bring honor to our husbands. Honor our husbands! You must be kidding! I can hear you now, "My husband does not deserve honor. He never helps with the kids. He leaves his stinky socks on the floor. He never tells me he loves me." Maybe your husband does not deserve your honor, but God does. The real truth lies in what honors God. You have to put Him first and ask Him to help you love your husband the way He commands. Love is a choice. It is often undeserved. God loves us and we know we do not deserve it. Ask God to help you find the love that you had for your husband when you first met. Even in the midst of the dirty socks and the sports pages your husband still deserves your admiration and love. Ladies what he really wants to know is that you love him above all others. Just think how you will knock his socks off when you act like the *Proverbs 31* woman. He won't recognize you. You will be a new woman, the woman God wants you to be. We have heard it before, but we have to practice it.

Some years ago, I had to do this very thing. I did not feel much love for my husband. I resented him and I felt that God had forsaken me. His command was clear. *Love as I have loved you.* I began to pray that God would help me to love my husband the way I did when we first met. I did not pray that God would change him, but rather that God would change me and He did. It was a gradual change. Even my husband recognized it.

I wish I could say that through this journey my life was like Snow White's or Cinderella's and that I lived happily ever after; but I did not. After twenty-three years of marriage, it ended in a divorce. I had a lot of trouble accepting the fact that I had a failed marriage, and I asked many questions. One thing remained crystal clear to me: it was not my job to change him; I had to allow God to do that, He could, however, change me and the way I saw my husband. The responsibility for changing your husband is not yours. This belongs to God. We must remember that. We cannot change our husband's heart, his bad habits or his desires. Only God can do that. Our response to him must be one of genuine love and concern for his spiritual and physical well-being. Sometimes it may take years, but if you are faithful to God, He will take care of your heart. There may be circumstances in which your husband will not yield to the call of God on his heart. It is then that you will need to try to resolve any issues by seeking help from your pastor or a Christian counselor. You begin by letting God work on you and see what happens.

There is a woman in the Bible who exemplifies the *excellent* woman. Her name is Ruth. If you are unfamiliar with the story, Ruth's husband died and so did his brother, leaving Ruth and her sister-in-law, Orpah *(not Oprah)*, to take care of their mother-in-law, Naomi. Let us look at what life must have been like for Ruth.

There was a vale of sadness that day; the day that Naomi had to approach the two most important people in her life. They were her daughters-in-law, Ruth and Orpah. Their husbands had died and left Ruth and Orpah to care for her, and she wasn't going to place that burden on them any longer. The three of them tried to make it on their own, but it was getting more and more difficult. Naomi had made arrangements to go to the people of her husband, (who had also died), and stay with them. She would release Ruth and Orpah even though it was going to break her heart to see them go. It wasn't fair to ask them to remain with her. Naomi drew up all the courage she had and asked God for the strength to let them go.

Ruth and Orpah loved Naomi and had worked very hard since the death of their husbands, but they knew that it was going to be impossible for them to continue to care for her with very little money and no family to help them. They had been trying to find ways to get the things they needed, but the money was quickly used up, and now they didn't know quite what they were going to do. Ruth and Orpah had not discussed this with each other nor with Naomi. In their hearts, they knew that soon they would be forced to leave the place they had called home.

As Naomi approached, she saw Ruth and Orpah taking what little flour they had to make cakes for their evening meal. Ruth saw her first, dusted the flour from her hands, and ran out to greet her mother-in-law. She loved Naomi as if she were her own mother. Since her husband's death, no one meant more to her than Naomi. When they met, they embraced one another and Ruth ushered Naomi inside and offered her a cool cup of water. Orpah, realizing that Ruth was no longer there; turned to find Naomi and Ruth seated at the table, Naomi's face was looking deeply trouble.

"Come here Orpah, I have something I must share with you and Ruth," was all that Naomi could say, choking back tears that threatened to spill out and down her cheek at any moment. Orpah wiped the flour from her hand, came, and sat down beside Naomi taking her hands in hers. She noticed that Naomi's hands were small in hers; yet they were still strong as she held Oprah's hand tightly. "What is wrong, mother?" Ruth asked fighting back her own tears. Naomi let go of one of Orpah's hands and reached over and took Ruth's hand and began to tell them of her decision to leave their home and go to live with her husband's family. The tears could not be stopped as she shared how much she loved both Ruth and Orpah. They were young and still able to remarry and have a family, and she could not bear watching them struggle to take care of her any longer. She would release them of any further responsibility to her, and they were free to return to their own families.

Orpah's face was without expression as she considered Naomi's words. It was almost a relief. She and Ruth had just this morning been talking about what was to become of them. Now she was free to return to her family, but something in her heart compelled her to want to stay with this woman who had been like a mother to her for ten years. She could not leave. They would find a way somehow, to stay together and through her tears she voiced a protest. "No, my mother, we will stay with you."

Ruth was stunned at Naomi's words, never had she even considered such a thing. Naomi was her family. Her resolve was strong and she moved close to Naomi. Orpah came along side her as well. Both were determined to stay with Naomi, but she was resolute, this was the only way. She urged her two daughters-in-law to return to their homeland when finally Orpah relented. She loved Naomi, but she wanted to go home. She leaned forward, kissed Naomi on the cheek, and rose to return to her people. Naomi urged Ruth to do the same, but Ruth clung to Naomi, "Do not urge me to leave you or to turn away, for wherever you go I will go, where you lodge I will lodge, your people will be my people and your God will be my God." Naomi saw that Ruth was determined to remain with her and said no more on the matter.

When they arrived at the home of Boaz, Naomi's husbands relative, there was relief and an overwhelming sense of God's goodness. Ruth, most of all, wanted to let it be known that she was able to work to care for Naomi. She asked Naomi for permission to work in the barley fields. Naomi knew this girl was a rare jewel and granted her permission to glean the fields behind the reapers for any barley that was left behind.

Ruth had no idea that the field she had been working in belonged to Boaz, but Boaz took notice of her. Her determination and her beauty pulled at his heart, and he instructed those working his fields to leave extra grain on the ground for Ruth. Ruth had found favor with Boaz and she had noticed that he was attending to her. She knew she did not deserve his attention; after all, she was not his family. Why was he helping her? Days went by and Boaz's attention became more evident. Ruth questioned him, "Why have I found favor with you?" she asked. .

Boaz was even more taken with this woman standing in his fields, her hands and face dirty from the dust that had blown on her from the fields, and he replied, "Because I have seen what you have done for you mother-in-law."

Boaz's love for Ruth continued to grow, as did Ruth's love for Boaz. Boaz was a wealthy man, and as was the custom, of their people, he sought to redeem Ruth since she was the daughter-in-law of Naomi, the wife of his relative. Boaz professed his love before the elders and took Ruth for his bride. Ruth conceived and bore a child whose name was Obed, the father of Jesse, the father of David. (Let me encourage you to read the Book of Ruth for the entire story of this remarkable woman.)

God often rewards us when we turn our hearts toward Him. How do I know? Ruth's life was like a fairy tale, but not just another Cinderella story. I am living proof that God delights in blessing his children; for when I felt alone, He was with me, and when I found my sufficiency in Him He gave me someone else to love.

Who wouldn't want to be that kind of woman, a woman of excellent character? It is possible to be that kind of woman. We have Ruth's example to guide us. It is my desire to be seen by my husband as a woman of excellent character. In the world today, we have women who have risen to high positions in our government, in the corporate world, and in the world of entertainment who, by the world's standards, are considered women of greatness. They have done many good things; there is no denying that. You can turn on the TV and hear about them or read about them in newspapers and magazines. You can also read about how they have lied and deceived the people they serve. Their lives reflect their true character. If we are going to pattern our lives after someone, shouldn't we be looking to the One who created us for the best role model?

Young women today need to have role models who reflect Christ-likeness. They need to see that it is possible to be a woman of excellent character, someone who is not willing to compromise the truth, one who believes in the sanctity of human life and a commitment to marriage, who practices the truth of God's word daily in her life.

If you want others to consider you a jewel, then you must be an "imitator of Christ and walk in love just as Christ has loved you".[4] You must have good moral character. Do not let your talk be unbecoming of a lady. Walk in goodness, righteousness, and truth. Do not participate in the things of the world that are ungodly. Give thanks to the Lord making most of your days in a way that is pleasing to God. "Wives, understand and support your husband in ways that support Christ."[5] Lift him up and pray for him daily that he will be the man of God he needs to be, and most important of all, love God.

For those of you, who are not yet married, know that a man wants his wife to possess these characteristics. Practice these things in your life now so that when the time comes God will honor you by giving you the man he has set apart for you, a man who is subject to God and is willing to lay down his life for you.

There is a misconception that men are after only one thing– sex. However, deep in his heart, a man wants to be loved. How do I know? I just had to ask my husband. Sex without love is just sex, but when a man feels completely loved by you then sex becomes the outward expression of that love.

Women seem to think that men do not really need to be shown love. Your husband finds his greatest needs fulfilled in knowing that he is loved. That is not the only thing he needs and we will talk about that in other chapters. My husband and I often talk about the differences between men and women and what I hear him say overwhelmingly to me is that he just

---

4 Ephesians 5:1-16, The New American Standard Bible, ©1960, 1962, 1968, 1971, 1972, 1973, 1975, 1977 by the Lockman Foundation, Used by permission.

5 Ephesians 5:22, *THE MESSAGE* is quoted: "scripture taken from *THE MESSAGE*. Copyright © 1993, 1994, 1995,1996,2000,2001, 2002. Used by permission of NavPress Publishing Group."

needs to know that I think he is the greatest man God has ever created. If he knows I think this about him then he will do anything to make me happy. My job is simple, love him and if I do that, then he will find me a jewel, a prized possession. I want to add a little footnote here as well, we must love God first before we can ever begin to really love our husbands.

DIGGING DEEPER:

1. Do I bring honor or my husband in my words and actions?

    Yes_____ No_____ Sometimes_____✓_____

    Look up the word **honor** in the dictionary and write down its meaning. _honesty in one's beliefs and action; high respect or public esteem_

    Read Philippians 4:8-9. What is the result of being honorable? The _peace_ of God will be with you.

2. Read the following passage of scripture, Matthew 22:37. What does it say about how we are to love God? _with all my heart, soul, and mind_

3. The Greek word for imitator is *mimetes*, which is where we get our word mimic. Read the following scripture Ephesians 5:1. Who are we to imitate? _God_

4. Think about ways that you can show support for your husband and list those here. _not interrupting him, remembering little things, pray for him, encourage him, show love by his love language_

5. Do you pray for your husband? _yes - sometimes_

   Read the following scriptures and pray them back to God, adding your husband's name to each verse.

   Proverbs 4:12, Proverbs 3:24, Psalm 1. Read Proverbs 6:16-19 and list the seven things God hates. _abomination, haughty eyes, lying tongue, hands that shed innocent blood, heart that devises wicked schemes, feet that are quick to rush to evil, false witness that pours out lies, person who stirs us conflict_
   Now pray and ask the Lord to protect your husband from those seven _in the community_ things.

PRAY THIS PRAYER:

Lord, increase my desire to become a woman of character and that my husband will find me a jewel among women. I know You want to see me blossom into a woman of beauty. Lord, You created me and want to show me off to the world as the wonderful woman I long to become.

Design # 2
"THE TRUST FACTOR"

Proverbs 31:11 - The heart of her husband trusts in her, and he will have no lack of gain.

Trust, we all want to be trusted and to trust our husbands. The idea here is that the excellent woman is trustworthy and the husband of such a woman lacks nothing. We learn two things about her from this verse first; the heart of her husband trusts her. He has confidence in his wife. Secondly, she is able to manage the family's income so that they are lacking nothing. I think the idea we see here is one of discipline. The Proverbs 31 woman is trustworthy and disciplined in the matter of finances.

We must take this matter very seriously, ladies. When we take our vows on our wedding day, they are not just words without meaning. They are vows we are making to our spouse before God. We are not to recite words and then forget about them.

Right now you are probably asking yourself, *"Just what did I say to him that day? It's been so long ago that I have forgotten."* Maybe you need to renew your commitment to your husband to reaffirm to him that you are going to be faithful and trustworthy.

On Valentine's Day, 2005, my husband and I attended a Covenant Marriage Seminar hosted by our then Governor, Mike Huckabee. As we arrived at the arena where the seminar was held, we were greeted by jeers and chants from Gay Rights activists and other protestors who were against the very idea that God had ordained the marriage of a man and a woman.

There were 6500 people from all over the state who attended the event, along with noted authors Dennis Rainey, Dr. Crawford Loritts, and singer CeCe Winans. We listened as they talked about the commitment a man and a woman make to each other when they get married. At the end of the seminar, the governor and his wife renewed their vows to each other in front of the 6500 people in attendance, and then in turn the husbands and wives who were there stood to their feet and renewed their vows to each other. We went through the traditional wedding vows again stating our pledge to honor and cherish one another in sickness and health until death parts us.

The men recited the vows first then the women, in turn, recited vows to their husbands. We got to the part about wives being submissive to their husbands and I (in jest) stopped and looked at him and shook my head, "Submit, are you serious; I am not going to submit. I am a 21st Century woman and I don't submit to anyone!" We laughed and my husband said if you don't say it then none of it means anything. Of course, I submitted and recited the vows. It was funny to us, but the truth is, sometimes I have trouble being submissive. I am an independent woman, but I have learned there are many things that I need to be less *independent* and more *submissive* about. Today that word makes the hair on the back of women's necks rise up and almost shout out I am NOT going to be submissive. It is not stated in many marriage vows. Submission does not mean subservient. My husband knows that I am committed to him. He also knows that I may struggle at times with issues like submission. My head may tell me to that I don't have to be submissive but my heart is to be what God wants me to be.

What is submission and why do I need to be submissive? In the days when Paul wrote the passage where we find this act of submission, (Ephesians 5:22), women in the pagan culture were seen as inferior, to be seen and not heard. The modern world outside Christianity would describe it as being under the authority of the husband, speaking only when spoken to. There are still cultures today that adhere to this belief. What does it really mean? Does it really mean that women are under the authority of the man, and he has the right to lord his position over the woman? No, not at all. As seen in this passage of text taken from the Teacher's Commentary:

"The Christian view is quite different. Women are seen as persons of equal worth and value. In the structure of society, men are given the role of head of the house, a role affirmed by God in this passage. Their headship is modeled on the way Christ loved the church, not on human systems of authority. This headship focuses attention on the way a "superior" is called to serve the "subordinate"! Specifically, Ephesians 5:27 which portrays Christ as giving Himself up for the church "to present her to Himself as a radiant church, without stain or wrinkle or any other blemish, but holy and blameless." In pursuit of this ministry, Christ nourishes and cares for the church. In the same way, husbands are to nurture their wives, seeking always to help the wife grow as a person and as a Christian.[6]

Your husband is the "House-band". The name *husband* comes from two root words: *Hus-* meaning household, shelter, dwelling and *band-* meaning something that binds, spiritually, morally, and legally[7]. He is to be the glue that holds the family together, the "house-bander". When you see your husband this way you can understand that he wants to protect and care for what is his. When Christ showed his love for the church and gave himself up for her this became the example men were to live by concerning their wives. What woman wouldn't find it easy to submit to her husband when he loves her like that? In the same way, the bride of Christ is to submit to His authority. We also must submit to the leadership and authority given to our husbands by God. He need not worry about your commitment to him or your love for him if you are following God's directive for your life.

I must also be a good steward with our finances. I work outside the home like many of you. We live in a society of two-income families. Very few families exist today where the wife stays at home and cares for the children. I applaud young women who are able to stay at home. You and your husband must make this choice together. What does God desire for you and your family? I am not suggesting that the Godly woman is a woman who stays at home or that in order to be a Proverbs 31 woman you must be a stay-at-home mom. God needs all of us to do different

---

6   Richards, L., & Richards, L.O. 19876. The Teacher's Commentary. Includes index. Victor Books: Wheaton, Ill.

7   Strong, J. 1996. *The exhaustive concordance of the Bible: Showing every word of the test of the common English version of the canonical books, and every occurrence of each word in regular order.* (electronic ed.). Woodside Bible Fellowship.: Ontario

things. Can you be a Proverbs 31 woman and work outside the home? Of course you can. Just because I am earning a portion of the income does not mean that I am free to spend it any way I want. I know women who have separate checking accounts from their husbands. They have bills they pay with their paychecks, and he has bills he pays with his paycheck, then what is left is theirs to spend. I think this is a bad idea. I am not saying that having a separate checking account is wrong, but when you divide the household expenses this way, there is no accountability between you. I strongly suggest that if you must have separate accounts that you make certain that what is yours is his and vice versa. Far too often, we want to lay claim to the money. I know I have done the same thing.

A few years ago, my husband had to be off work due to an illness so I took a second job to help with the finances. It was only going to be for a short period, but even after he returned to work, I continued with the second job. That short period turned into years and during that time, I felt that I controlled that extra income. I worked for it and it was mine. I put away most of the money, but if I wanted to buy something, I felt free to do so. However, if my husband wanted the money for something, I was reluctant to give it to him. I was stingy with it. This was wrong. We are partners, and as partners what is mine is his. I shouldn't hoard that money as if it were mine alone. I soon realized that what I had worked so hard for I was becoming a slave to it. Soon I dreaded the time I had to spend doing that job. It was not worth the extra money I was bringing home, so I quit. It was the best decision I could have made. Do I miss the extra money? Sometimes, but the time I have with my family is much more important than the little extra income. God will honor your decisions when they line up with his will for your life.

There must be balance where finances are concerned. God expects us to be wise with what we He has given us. We are not always going to do the right thing. We need to make an effort to live within our means. This is so very hard in today's society. Everywhere we look, we see big new homes, fancy new cars, and info-mercials on TV about how to get rich and live the American Dream. Many couples struggle in this area. I am no different. We all want financial security. Who wouldn't like a never-ending six-figure balance in their checking account? God wants you to be free, debt free, because He knows if you are consumed with debt then you cannot fully live for Him. For most American's we have some debt, so don't beat yourself up here. Ideally, the best way to live is without creating debt. If you have debt, and most of your will have some, you must make sure that you are not living outside of your financial means.

To be a "virtuous" woman you must do your part to make sure that the finances you and your husband earn are not misused. If your husband pays the bills, don't make it hard on him to come up with enough money to cover the bills. Be informed. Ask questions. Show interest there. You need to know. If you pay the bills, enlist your husband's input. He needs to feel that you are trustworthy in this area, that the bills are paid on time and that you <u>both</u> are being good stewards with your money.

Now, if you are single how does this apply to you? When you handle finances as a single person in a godly way then the man God, may one day bring into your life as your life mate, will be confident that he can trust you seeing how you have managed your finances as a single woman. I have a single son, and I am praying that when the time comes God will bring a woman such as this into his life, one who will compliment him, encourage him and be a helpmate to him in areas of finance as well as other areas. I have seen too often young couples get into trouble because one or both of them do not know how to handle their finances. More marriages break up because of money than any other reason. It is a very stressful area of marriage, and we need to work together to make it a success.

I want us to take look at another a Proverbs 31 woman in the Bible. This woman's name is Abigail. Unfortunately, for Abigail, she did not have a loving husband. We find in this Biblical account that a confrontation takes place between some servants of David and Abigail's husband, Nabal. Let's see how Abigail fits the Proverbs 31 role of a trustworthy wife.

David, who was known as the "slayer of giants", was living in the wilderness of Paran. He was aware of a rich man Nabal, who had a flock of 3000 sheep. David had been living peaceably among them. Nabal's servants were working in Carmel and David noticed the men, but did not bother them. He was a powerful man, but desired to live in peace with his neighbor.

David gathered his servants together and gave them instructions "Go to the camp of Nabal and to visit him in my name. Say to him, "peace be with you, your house and all that you have." David then placed a hand on the shoulders of his men and smiled, "Tell him that we have seen his shearers in Carmel and have let them live in peace among us, then ask for his favor to be on you. In kindness we come and request that you share your bread and water with us". David blessed the men and sent them out.

Abigail stood next to the well dropping the pail into the refreshing water below. It was another hot day and like the sheep on the hillside, which stood next to the stream dipping their heads into it for a cool drink of water, she too was thirsty for a drink.

Off in the distance Abigail could see some men coming across the dusty dry land so she waited by the well as they approached. Nabal was shearing one of his prized rams and he too noticed the men coming closer. "Go inside," he shouted at Abigail. Nabal was an angry man. He often said hurtful things to her and she was accustomed to his outbursts. Not wanting to hear anything more, she set down the pail of water and headed back inside her home.

As the men approached, Nabal stood his ground firm. He was not known for hospitality, and he had no use for vagabonds and beggars.

"Good day sir, may the Lord bless you kindly," the men said as they drew closer to Nabal.

"What is it you want?" were the only words that Nabal offered in response to them.

These men were servants of David and had come a long way in need of bread and water and had hoped to find kindness among the men in Nabal's camp, but there was no kindness here. Nabal had never heard of anyone named David or his father, Jesse. He wasn't going to believe them because he had had his own servants leave him. Why should he believe they were servants of this man named David? Nabal quizzed the men standing by the well for what seemed like an eternity, but he was not impressed in the least by these men of David's.

Nabal refused to give any bread or water to David's servants cursing them and saying, "should I take the bread and water away from my own servants and give them to a man I know nothing about; I don't think so." Nabal's name meant fool and this he was. He had no idea what was about to happen as a result from his actions. The men turned and headed back to their camp to report to David what had taken place.

David was outraged as the men recounted the story of how Nabal had refused them any bread or water. He decided that he would take matters into this own hands and that Nabal would pay for such a refusal. "Tell the men who are with us to take up their swords and follow me, we will see how Nabal feels about refusing me". David had an army of 600 men and he took 400 of them with him leaving 200 to stay behind and guard their camp.

Nabal had no idea that David was a powerful man. He did not know that David was an anointed servant of Jehovah, God of Abraham and Isaac. He knew nothing of David slaying the giant with just a sling and a stone. However, today he was going to find out.

David did not know that Nabal had a wife named Abigail, but one of his servants had seen her as they approached and he decided to go on ahead of David and his army to warn her that David was coming to kill her husband.

Abigail was unaware of what had transpired between those men and her husband. She was not about to question Nabal when she saw that he had turned them away without so much as a cup of water. Seeing that he had gone up the hillside to tend his flock of sheep, she decided it would be safe enough to return to the well. She had left the pail sitting there and she needed water for their supper. As she was returning to the house she saw one of the men who had been there earlier returning. This time he was running and he was alone. She recognized him by the clothing that he was wearing. She was not afraid so she waited until he came near. "Who is it you are looking for? My husband has gone to take care of his sheep," she questioned the young man who was gasping for a breath as he stood in front of her.

"I am a messenger from David. We were here earlier to ask for some bread and water for our men. We have been camped among your shepherds for some time now but we have left them alone. David is a mighty warrior, but we did not come to this region to bring any harm to you or your husband, however your husband refused to give any assistance and this made David very angry. He has ordered 400 of his men to come here and destroy every living thing. You do not know what kind of man my master is and he will show no mercy."

Abigail thought carefully for a moment and then responded to the young man standing in front of her. There was no time to consult Nabal and she knew that he would not be the least bit afraid for her safety. She instructed the young man to help her gather all the bread and wine that she had stored in the house (which was about 200 loaves of bread and two jugs of wine.) "Help me gather some corn and figs and these clusters of grapes," she said as she worked quickly to get all these things together. Time was very important and she did not intend to leave anything behind that she might be able to use to persuade David not to kill her or her husband. She loaded the packs on donkeys and headed for David's camp. As she was coming across the hidden part of the hillside, she spotted David and he spotted her. Her heart began to beat in her chest so loud that it almost drowned out the voice of David, as she got closer to him.

He called out to her, "What has brought you here?" Abigail recalled her conversation with his servant and offered David the bread and other provisions she had brought and requested that he have mercy on her ignorant, foolish husband.

Abigail risked her life in the wilderness. She did not do it for Nabal. She did it for their servants and their servant's families. She had to try to win David's favor, and she did. She remembered hearing of David's defeat against the giant and how she had heard his name mentioned among their servants. She knew that he could and would have no problem killing them all if he wanted to. She had to try.

So impressed was David with this woman that he agreed for her sake to accept her offering. Abigail had managed to save Nabal and their servants, but now she had to tell him what she had done and she knew that he would not be happy with her. He had told her many times that he did not need any woman fighting his battles for him. How in the world would she explain this to him? She could just not tell him, he would never know. She knew that she had to tell him, she could not keep this a secret.

When Abigail arrived home, she found Nabal had returned from working in the field and was having a party. He was very drunk. She knew that if she told him what had happened he wouldn't believe her so rather than talk to a drunken fool, she decided to wait until the morning when he would be sober and able to understand what she told him. She prayed. All night she prayed that God would be with her in the morning as she faced the wrath of Nabal.

When daylight came, Abigail found Nabal and recalled the story of how she had met David and offered him bread and wine for their safety. Nabal's heart died within him. How could she do such a thing? He turned away from her and his heart became like a stone towards her. Abigail was not sorry for what she had done. Nabal's anger was no surprise either, but she did what she felt she had to do, Nabal would never have sought forgiveness from David or her. For the next ten days, Nabal refused to speak to Abigail, and the Lord struck him dead.

David, hearing of Nabal's death, praised God for His goodness and sent his servants to the house of Abigail. They found her there and told her that David had seen in her a woman who could be trusted with many things and this pleased him very much. Now that she was a widow, he wanted to make her his wife and he did. (You can read the story of Abigail in 1 Samuel chapter 25)

This story has a happy ending. It sounds more like a movie script than a story from the Bible. A good woman is married to a bully. A hero comes along. The bully of a husband dies. The hero takes the woman to be his wife and they live happily ever after. Often reality does not play out quite that way. God wants us to be trustworthy no matter what the circumstances are. You see, God was in charge of this situation. It was God who required payment for Nabal's greed and his arrogance, not Abigail. She did not take his life. God did. What can we learn from her?

How about the time you bought a new pair of shoes, but you were afraid to tell your husband so you hid them from him. When he finally asked you about them, you told him, "Oh, these old shoes, I've had them for a long time". Truthfully, you only bought them a few weeks ago. Were you afraid to tell him that you bought the shoes because he would get mad? Many women have issues with this sort of thing. They are in no position to buy anything without their husband's approval. So in order to get what they want without their husband making a scene, they choose to hide it from him for as long as possible. Many times, we are caught in the trap of dishonesty not really meaning to, but out of fear of being made to feel that we have done something wrong; therefore, we just do not say anything about it. I have done it and maybe you have too. This does not fit the model of the Proverbs 31 woman. Now here is where you might say she just could not be a real person. She is far too perfect. Maybe she is not real, but God saw fit to give us a guide through his Word so that we could work towards becoming a woman like that.

Does your husband have your loyalty to him in other areas as well? What about your children? Does your husband know what you are teaching your children? The scriptures tell us to "train up a child in the way that he should go". You both have to agree on how you are going to raise your children. One parent cannot go against the other parent and undermine what he or she is doing. Ladies, you need to support your husband in this area. Pray for him and pray for yourself that God's word will guide you in areas of discipline and instruction.

It is very important that you and your husband reach an agreement when you have a difference of opinion. I can say from personal experience that when you disagree your children will know it. They can tell when the parents are not working together for their good. Too often one parent will walk away and let the other parent deal with the children. A Proverbs 31 woman is not a woman who is raising the children alone. She is raising the children under the leadership of the father. We can never take away what God has intended the home to represent. The father is to be the head of the home, and the mother is to be the love of his life. Children will see that and will respect both parents when they see that their parents love each other. Wives, let your children see that you respect their father and that you are working together for their benefit. There is always going to be the need for balance in the area of discipline. Many families have been at great odds over this particular area.

Wives also need to have a good reputation and conduct themselves in such a way as to be pleasing to their husbands and to God. I cringe sometimes when I see the way some woman dress. They speak volumes without saying a word. I wonder what their husbands think when they dress provocatively. We need to bring honor to our husbands by dressing modestly. I don't mean you have to wear a dress to the ground and a turtleneck. However, I do suggest that you be careful that your appearance is not causing some other man than your husband to sin by lusting in his heart because you have not chosen to dress appropriately.

Your husband needs to be proud of you. So don't look fifteen years older than you are and don't look fifteen years younger either. Get up in the morning, get dressed, put on your makeup and fix your hair. Not only will you feel better but your husband will like it too! Women need to take care of themselves. Don't let yourself go. I never leave my house without being dressed properly and having my makeup and hair done. Why, because it makes me feel good about myself and I want to please my husband. I want him to think he has a beautiful wife, even if I am not the most beautiful woman in the world. I want him to think I am, and if I do not care about the way I look then what is he going to do. He is going to look at someone else. While I am on this soapbox let me say this to the mothers of young teenage girls. Don't let peer pressure and TV advertising cause you to give in to their demands to look like everyone else. I am appalled at the way some of the young girls dress today. They are leaving nothing to the imagination! God created your daughters to be loved and respected. When they dress inappropriately, men will neither love, nor respect them. Moms, do not let your daughters dress in a way that leaves some young man with the wrong idea about your daughter. Be a good example for her.

Whether you are married or single, you should delight in being a woman of virtue. Your husband and your future husband, if you are single, will delight in you too.

DIGGING DEEPER:

1. Read the following verses on trust: Proverbs 3:5, Isa. 25:3, Psalm 37:3

2. Read Luke 14:28. For which of you desiring to build a tower, does not _____ and _____ the _____ whether he has _____ to complete it.

3. Are you disciplined in matters of finance? On a scale of one to ten where do you think you fit?

   1-------|-------|-------|-------|-------|-------|-------|-------|-------10

4. Look up the word respect in the dictionary. Write that definition below: _____

   _____

   _____

   Proverbs 19:14 says-- A house of _____ are inherited from fathers but a _____ wife is from the Lord.

5. Read 1 Peter 31:1, 1 Peter 3:5, and Eph. 5:21-22. The key word in these

passages is _____. What is your husband's response
to be towards you (Eph. 5:25)? _____

_____

_____

PRAY THIS PRAYER:

Lord, as I go through this day may Your words ring loud and clear in my
ear. May I become a woman whose husband trusts her. Help me Lord, to
make the right choices. Let me see my husband through Your eyes. To love
and respect him so that I may bring honor to You.

Design #3

"WAR AND PEACE"

Proverbs 31:12 - She does him good and not evil all the days of her life.[8]

In the world today, we find a great deal of evil; it is all over the newspapers and on television. The news media seems to thrive on these stories about the evil in the world. In July 2006, the focus in the news media was on an area in the world where one nation was testing rockets capable of delivering nuclear warheads to the United States. We are and have been at war with other nations who have sought to rob us of our freedoms. Not only is our own country fighting a war, but also around the world, war is going on in many places. How are we to keep peace in our families in times of war?

What does your home look like? Does it look like there has been a war going on? Do you and your husband shoot rockets at each other, verbally or with "looks that could kill"? If you do, then you are neither honoring your husband, nor doing him good all of your life.

Have you ever been around the military? I have. I was raised in a military family. My father was in the Air Force for over twenty years and I learned to have a great sense of pride for what our military does. I have a son who has now chosen to serve his country as his grandfather did further making my chest swell with pride. I boast a proud license plate cover proclaiming that I am an *Air Force Parent*.

Last fall I attended the annual Air Show at the military base close to our home. Once I walked through the gates of the base, it brought back

8   The New American Standard Bible

many memories of my youth, living on that exact base. At the time I lived there, I did not really appreciate what it was that my father was doing there. It was just my life. I did not really care for it at the time. Because we moved around quite a lot during those years, I thought that my parents were robbing me of the memories made with lifelong friends. To tell the truth those were character building years, whether I lived in the same town all my life or moved every two or three years.

Keeping peace has been a practice among the military for centuries, but there are times when action is required --decisive action. Our country was (and still is) founded on the principles of fairness and goodness, never evil. When we chose to go after the men responsible for the bombing of the Twin Towers and crashing planes with hundreds of innocent people on them, it was in response to evil, not flexing our muscles at the world to say we are the "superpower of the world."

Webster defines peace this way:

*1: a state of tranquility or quiet: as **a**: freedom from civil disturbance **b**: a state of security or order within a community provided for by law or custom <a breach of the peace*

2: freedom from disquieting or oppressive thoughts or emotions

3: harmony in personal relations

*4 **a**: a state or period of mutual concord between governments*

b: a pact or agreement to end hostilities between those who have been at war or in a state of enmity

5 — used interjectionally to ask for silence or calm or as a greeting or farewell.[9]

Our nation seeks to bring peace to other parts of the world where there is no peace. While our mission at times is uncertain, peace is always the objective. There are those in the world who would seek to destroy us because of what we stand for. Our men and women are fighting to preserve that freedom that we so lavishly enjoy. We dare those who would threaten our way of life to try to come in and destroy it.

We are to be the peacemakers in our homes. Our homes should be a haven of refuge for all who reside there. Our families need to be able to come home to a place where love and respect is the norm. Peacemakers are

---

9   Merriam-Webster, Inc: *Merriam-Webster's Collegiate Dictionary.* 10th ed. Springfield, Mass., U.S.A. : Merriam-Webster, 1996, c1993

the ones who bring peace by reconciliation to opposing parties. We read in the Bible, "blessed are the peacemakers" i.e. *happy* are the peacemakers. Living in a state of happiness is much more enjoyable than living in a state of discontent.

There was a time early in my marriage that Jim and I were trying to figure out each other. I really didn't know his temperament and he didn't really know mine. I was (and still am) very independent. I had learned to be that way through some difficult times in my life. Jim has a strong temperament as well. When we had our first real disagreement, Jim was ready to throw in the towel. During our disagreement, I thought it was better to walk away and let him cool off---bad idea! I didn't realize that Jim was the type of person who the longer you let him "alone" to think, the worse it got. He wanted me to reconcile. I wanted him to sweat a little. He wanted me to throw my arms around him and talk gently to him. I did not want to talk to the walking volcano. That was asking too much. I thought that when you reached the boiling point you just needed to turn off the heat and let it cool. Now that I know he wants me to discuss things with him, even if our viewpoints are different, I can be more of a peacemaker, if the need arises. Thankfully, it does not happen very often.

We can look back at it now and laugh but at the time, it was no laughing matter. Someone had to give and we just had to decide who it was going to be. Believe me, it was a long few hours of both of us standing our ground in the situation. In the end, someone had to make peace. Truthfully, I don't remember who it was. We had made a commitment and we believed that God brought us together. We had to ask God to intervene and help us work through those early days to keep us focused on what was important to us.

It is therefore to be our mission in life to be peacemakers, to bring good, not evil to our husbands and children. As I write this chapter, I am reminded of those times in my own life when I was not a very good peacemaker. I remember telling my children when they would argue with each other that they should be peacemakers. I would ask each of them to decide who it was going to be, which one of them would step up and be the peacemaker in the situation. Most of the time neither one of them really wanted to be the one to bring peace to the situation. That would signal defeat and they would rather stand their ground than give in to defeat. Why is it that we feel defeated when we back down or when we attempt to work towards a peaceful resolution to our problem? Most of our nature, the human part of us, doesn't want to bring a peaceful resolution to the situation. We would rather stand our ground and fight. When we become peacemakers, we become the conduit that God can use to reveal His mercy and grace. That grace and mercy can only come from Him and flow through us. Satan seeks to destroy that conduit to God by clogging up the whole thing with lies and deception.

When we seek to do good, not evil, it is not through our own humanness that this is accomplished. Why? When sin entered the world and evil began to run amuck, our very nature was evil because of that sin. The Holy Spirit living in us is the only way in which we could ever possibly "be good". It just is not our nature!

Remember the nursery rhythm, "There once was a little girl who had a little curl right in the middle of her forehead. When she was good she was very good, but when she was bad she was horrid." We are all that way---evil to the core and capable of being horrid. Not all will choose to be horrid; some will choose to be good in their own way, but without Christ all of that goodness is as filthy rages. There is no one who is "good" and "righteous" apart from Christ. It is Christ who makes us righteous. When we live apart from Christ, our "goodness" is self-serving. When we live in Christ, our "goodness" is Christ serving. We seek to do things that draw attention to ourselves when we live apart from Christ. When we live for Christ, we seek to draw attention to Him.

As a wife and mother it is my responsibility to speak well of my family. I have said and others have said as well, "Don't say anything bad about my family that is reserved for me." We take offense when others criticize our family. It brings us to our feet loaded and ready for a fight. Why? Because, no matter what they have done and where they are, they are still part of us and no one, *except us*, has the right to tear them down.

If we really believe that no one has that right to speak against our families, should we not also protect the way we treat and talk to them or about them. Ladies, when you are having lunch with the girls, guard what you say about your husband to others. Do not run him down and talk bad about him in front of them. This will show disrespect for your husband. Think about how you would feel if you knew that your husband was talking to his friends about last night's supper that you made and how that wasn't the best meal he has ever had, or about the few pounds you have put on since you got married. If we want our husbands to love us the way that Christ loved the church, then we need to lift him up and brag on him to our friends and family.

I want to share another little story with you about my husband. A few years ago I was helping a friend from work with a yard sale to raise money for her ill sister. It was a hot day and it was going to be a long day sitting outside. I had injured my back about six weeks prior to that and was facing surgery in just a few days. My husband didn't want me to carry or lift the heavy boxes, so he offered to come with me to the yard sale and help with setting the things out so that I would not do anything to further injure my back. Once things were set in place and people started to arrive, he could have gone home and done something that he wanted to do; instead, he chose to stay with me. He went and got everyone breakfast and helped people load things into their vehicles. Once the sale was over, he sent me home and he stayed to help put the things away. My friends saw him doing this and commented to me what I wonderful husband I had. I agree! I would never dream of tearing him down in front of others. When he shows me that he loves me by giving up his day to be with me in the hot sun, yard selling nonetheless, I would be less than virtuous, now wouldn't I, if I talked bad about him in front of my friends.

That is what it means, she does him good, not evil. This is to be an ongoing process. The scriptures tell us to practice this all the days of our lives. I am blessed to have Jim as my husband. I can tell you that it has not always been this way. I had to learn to practice this kind of virtue. When I was younger I was guilty of being mean-spirited. I talked with my girlfriends about the things that were going on at home, gaining support from them against my husband. If things weren't going well at home, it was nothing to share that with the girls at work. We all seemed to share the same thing. Problems were never in short supply. Someone was always having marriage problems. I don't remember a time when I heard the women bragging on their husbands. They didn't sit around and talk about the good things their husbands were doing. They were drawing on the negative. For the past thirty years that has not changed. I still hear young wives talking bad about their husbands. I challenge you to stop and look at the man you married with a different eye. Look at him through God's eyes. Ask yourself some hard questions.

First, ask yourself, "Why did I marry this man?" What was it that you saw in him that made you want to marry him? Has that changed? If so, why has it changed? It is you or him?

Secondly, ask yourself "what do I love about him?" There was something that made you love him in the first place. Those qualities are still there. Maybe you need to bring them out in him again. Men need to feel that they are loved. If you are not showing him respect, then you are not showing him love. You may feel that you have shown him love and respect but now he doesn't deserve it. Whatever the reason, you do what God wants you to do. You be the peacemaker; you be the one who lifts him up. You pray for him to be the man God wants, not the man *you* want.

I am telling you these things because I have lived them. I have been in the position of lifting up and tearing down. When you lift him up and he believes that you find him most desirable of all men, that you think he can move mountains, that you believe he is the most handsome of all men, then he will try to move mountains for you. He will think that you are a ten when you think you are a five. He will work yard sales with you on a hot June day. He will do the laundry and help with the kids. Why? Because you are the one who loves him--flaws and all. No one loves him the way you do. Why do men look elsewhere and why is there so much infidelity? Because, the wives aren't doing *him good*. Make him feel like a ten, even when his hair is getting thin and he is getting a little big around the middle. Ladies, you have the ability to make him want to be "superman" for you, and when he is willing to move that mountain for you don't you want to lift him up and *do good*.

We have examples in scripture of married women who loved their husbands and who have done him good. I love what King Solomon wrote about the woman he loved. In the first few verses of the Song of Solomon, the bride confesses her love. Let's look at these first few verses of chapter one together:

"May he kiss me with the kisses of his mouth!

For your love is better than wine.

Your oils have a pleasing fragrance,

Your name is *like* purified oil;

Therefore the maidens love you.

Draw me after you *and* let us run *together!*

The king has brought me into his chambers."[10]

This is obviously written by a woman in love! What impressed her was his character. In verse three, she says that his name is like purified oil. Comparing his name to a perfume meant that his character was pleasing to her. She speaks well of him, wouldn't you say? As we read the poetic form of these scriptures, it is obvious to the reader that the King is as smitten, as is his bride-to-be. Theirs is a mutual admiration for one another. He finds her exquisitely beautiful and she finds him the finest of all men. The theme throughout the book is love. It is a mushy love story. We women love mushy love stories. We want to be loved by our husbands the same way King Solomon loved his bride. The groom also wants to be loved like King Solomon's beloved. Read here what King Solomon says about his beloved:

"How beautiful you are, my darling

How beautiful you are!

Your eyes are *like* doves."[11]

To which she responds!

"My beloved is dazzling and ruddy,

Outstanding among ten thousand!"[12]

I love to read a good romance novel. I don't read the trashy novels but I enjoy reading Christian novels. I love to get wrapped up in their lives through the pages of each story. They always have a happy ending. The boy gets the girl and they live out their lives serving the Lord together. How perfect is that? A little too perfect. Our lives are not at all like those in the novels. Not everything always works out the way we planned. Sometimes we do not get the life we dreamed of having. Not always will the man you marry be like King Solomon. You may get Fred Flintstone and end up living in the dark ages. You may get George Jetson and live in the fast lane, on the go all the time.

Whatever your circumstances, there is hope. Hope that God can use your circumstance to bring about good for your marriage. Remember that

---

10 The New American Standard Bible

11 The New American Standard Bible, "Song of Solomon, chapter 4, verse 1

12 The New American Standard Bible, "Song of Solomon, chapter 5, verse 10

God is for you. He is for your marriage too. He wants to bring about good in your life. Let's start by making our husbands feel like King Solomon. He is the king of his house. You are his bride, and there was a reason the two of you got married. Let's get practical. Start where you are. Do something so show him that you appreciate him. You may have to start small. That's okay just start! If you have trouble thinking of something that he has done that you can praise him for, begin by thanking him for working so hard to provide for you and your children. We will get into this a little more as we study more about this virtuous woman. I hope that you will hang in there with me to the finish. It is going to be a journey worth taking.

Before we continue this journey together, let's look for a few moments at another Proverbs 31 woman. We have talked about her briefly in this chapter, but I want to explore her virtues a little deeper. She was the young Shulammite bride who fell in love with the king.

A young Shulammite woman was tending her sheep when a handsome nobleman took notice of her. Her hair was long and flowed softly around her face as she knelt down to pick up the small lamb and hold it close to her. She stroked it tenderly and cuddled it next to her as a loving mother would her child. Solomon watched her from a distance. He could not take his eyes off her. Her beauty was like none he had ever seen.

The young king called out to the servants who were tending to his every need. "Find out who that woman is for me," he commanded. His servants turned on their heels to do exactly as their master had bid them to do.

Across the way, this beautiful young maiden was dreaming of a young man. As she caressed the little lamb, her mind was wondering back to the handsome man whom she had been watching from a distance. She had seen him on many occasions; his arms were strong and he was as handsome a man as she had ever seen. She longed to know this man, but it seemed impossible. After all, he was the King. They came from two different worlds. "He would never notice her," she thought. Her mind was far way, she was brought back to reality by the sound of her friends giggling. They were talking to some young men near her father's stables. As they talked, one of the young men pointed towards the young Shulammite girl.

One of the maidens ran over to her and spoke with excitement, "The King wants to know your name!"

"Why? Had he been watching her too?" she thought. Her heart skipped a beat and she could hardly contain her joy.

The young men turned to carry word back to the King that they had found the woman he sought. Suddenly the young Shulammite woman was filled with anticipation. Was it possible that she would finally meet the man she had been dreaming of?

Weeks passed and Solomon's love for the young Shulammite woman grew stronger each day. Her love for him was undeniable. "How could this happen?" she thought. "We barely know each other yet I cannot bear being separated from him for even a moment." The King wanted more than anything to spend all his time with this exquisite woman whom he held in his arms, but he was the King after all, and his duties as King took him away from her far more than he desired..

She could not hold back the love she felt for him, and before he left she told him how she felt about him. "Oh, my love", she began as she pulled him close to her, "Kiss me and never stop, for your love is far better than wine. I love the smell of you and I know now why all the other women love you too. How is it that you would love someone like me? I work in my father's fields tending his sheep and my skin is dark, not fair like the other young maidens." She hung her head and a tiny tear fell to the ground.

Solomon's fingers touched her lips, "Don't you know how beautiful you are, your cheeks are set aglow from the settings in your earrings. Your necklace frames the curve of your neck. I cannot breathe when I am with you." Solomon pulled her close and kissed her passionately then turned to leave. He had to go but he could not bring himself to say goodbye; it was impossible.

Solomon was a man of God. God had blessed him because of his devotion to Him. He could not dishonor God by taking this woman to his home until he made her his bride. He was the King and he could have her with him forever if he so much as made a gesture to her. Again, he stopped his mind from such things. "I cannot," He pushed the thought of her away just for a time. He knew that theirs was a love that would burn forever. He would make her his bride and very soon.

Some time passed and the young Shulammite woman found herself counseling the other young women in her village about love and marriage. "Let me tell you how it was when Solomon went away," she recalled, as she gathered the young maidens close to her, each of them leaning in with anticipation. "I was so upset the day he left that I couldn't even fall asleep. I wandered the streets looking for him. I was so lost without him. The night watchmen saw me and asked me where I was going and what I was doing wandering the streets so late at night. I could only ask them to help me find my true love. As morning came I saw someone in the distance. It was him; it was my beloved. I would know him anywhere. He drove a carriage with sixty of his men surrounding him on all sides. It had to be him; my heart stopped. I could barely move. I had to will myself forward. When I did, I ran to him and threw my arms around his neck so tight I think he almost stopped breathing." The girls laughed and she continued with her story.

The young Shulammite woman stood up and moved towards the window, "Come and see him dressed for his wedding. Here is a man whose heart is bursting with joy. Come with me now as I prepare for my wedding day." The young girls helped the young Shulammite prepare herself to marry the man she had only dreamed of just a few short months ago. "God is good", she thought. "No God is great!"

The two became one in marriage that day. The wedding was the talk of the village. Never before had anyone witnessed such love between a man and a woman. Their love was a love that came from God and no one could deny it. (If you are unfamiliar with this woman, you can read about her in Song of Solomon.)

The picture we see here in not only a picture of two young lovers who cannot get enough of each other, but of a young couple whose love and devotion not only to each other but to God would help them overcome whatever life threw at them. She bragged on him and he bragged on her. We need to do that, ladies. We need to let others know how much he means to us. We need to do him good, not evil all the days of his life.

DIGGING DEEPER:

1. Can you recall the last time you bragged on your husband to your friends? What did you say? _____

   _____

   _____

2. Look up Matthew 5:9 and write it out here. _____

    _____

    _____

3. What are three character traits that your husband possesses that first
    drew you to him? _____

    _____

4. Read Song of Solomon 5:10-16 and pay close attention to the young
    bride's admiration for the bridegroom. List as many things as you
    find in those verses that express her feelings for the man she is going
    to marry. _____

    _____

    _____

    _____

    _____

5. Now, go back and circle those words that express the way you see your
    husband. (*If you are having trouble with this exercise now is a good time
    to ask the Lord to help you with this*)

PRAY THIS PRAYER:

Lord to help me to see my husband as You see him. Help me to love him
the way I did when we first met. Forgive me Lord if I have spoken words
of disrespect towards my husbands. Guard my mouth so that I do not tear
him down; rather give me words of encouragement to lift him up.

Design #4

"MARTHA STEWART LOOK OUT"

**Proverbs 31:13 - She looks for wool and flax,
And works with her hands in delight.**[13]

When you hear the name Martha Stewart what comes to your mind? The woman can probably make dirt taste good. She can take an ordinary idea and create something extraordinary with it. She has had her own TV show, her own magazine, her own line of household products, and she has her own troubles. While Martha Stewart is capable of creating a beautiful home, the question remains, is she a delight to her family? More importantly is she a delight to the Lord.

A few summers ago, Jim and I took a cruise for our anniversary. We were very excited about being onboard a beautiful cruise ship sailing into the glorious waters of the Caribbean. Our first stop was Montego Bay, Jamaica. We had seen pictures and heard stories about the beautiful, white, sandy beaches. With all that we had seen and heard, we were looking forward to seeing this magnificent city for ourselves. When the ship docked, the view was incredible. The water truly was sapphire blue and emerald green. We could not wait to get off the ship and experience Jamaica for ourselves.

When we left the ship, we were transported by bus to visit one of the local tourist attractions. As we boarded our bus for a TWO-HOUR ride to a waterfall, known as Dunns River Falls, a wild man drove us through

13 New American Standard

the local villages. There were no traffic signals, no highway signs, no stop signs, and no markings on the road. Nothing! It was a wild ride with a wild driver. We were tossed around in the bus like popcorn in the microwave as our driver traversed through narrow streets barely missing the pedestrians crossing the streets. We had a very good driver however, because he didn't hit a single person, although we were certain he would.

Our guide on the bus was a young Jamaican woman who had never been outside of her country. As we made our way through Jamaica she showed us points of interest, and we talked about how very different life was there. It was obvious to us that the only beautiful things in Montego Bay lie behind the walls of the gated resorts. On one side of the street were lush, green landscaped lawns with spectacular, floral gardens and magnificent resorts just behind the towering iron gates. On the opposite side of the street were small concrete homes, dilapidated old buildings, and a stark contrast to the resorts just across the street.

We made our way through small villages, as we did I noticed that many people were walking to the markets, some to buy, others to sell. It was a sea of dark skinned men and women who paid little attention to the American tour buses they were so accustomed to seeing passing through.

Upon arrival at Dunns River Falls, our guide warned us to stay away from the "market" when we made our way out of the falls. Apparently, the locals would try to sell unsuspecting Americans, like us, their goods for an outrageous price. Once Jim and I finished climbing the waterfall we were separated from the rest of the group. We could not see which direction the rest of our group had gone and, you guessed it, we found ourselves standing near the entrance of "*the market*" looking for a way to get back to the bus. We knew we were not supposed to go through there but the people seemed insulted that we thought we needed to avoid them. Shouting "why won't you come in, we won't hurt you." (*This by the way gave me little comfort*). Not wanting to insult anyone, or seem afraid of the villagers we decided to walk a little way inside the market area. This was not one of our better decisions, because once we were "*inside*" we were trapped. Now we **had** to walk through the market. The market was filled with people who were trying to sell their goods to anyone who was willing to buy them. We didn't really mind the fact that everyone wanted our business, but we couldn't buy from them all.

We finally made it back to the bus, and yes, we were the last to arrive. We were a little embarrassed because everyone on the bus was waiting for us and they all knew where we had been because we were carrying purchases we had made in the market. On our two-hour ride back to the cruise ship, we talked with our guide about the local merchants, and how their livelihood depended on what they would sell.

Life there was much different from life in the United States where we have shopping malls and grocery stores. However, I believe life in Jamaica was very similar to life during Biblical days where men and women would go to the marketplaces to buy and sell. In Jamaica, the marketplace was where all the buying and selling took place for the smaller villages. There were a few stores but no malls. They have the open-air markets, and we have Kroger. They have sidewalk vendors; we have J.C. Penney's and Sears.

The virtuous woman in Proverbs 31:13 is diligent in caring for her family's physical needs, buying such things as food and clothing. (*You see women are natural-born shoppers*). The first thing we notice about her in this passage is that she *looks* or searches for wool and flax. She is frugal. She does not just buy the first thing she finds, she is a bargain hunter. (*The word frugal or furgalis in Latin means virtuous.*) She is also going to make the families clothes.

I have a friend who is an exceptional seamstress. She can make anything, and she does not even need a pattern. She just knows what to do. (*I can barely hem a pair of pants or sew on a button*). I have another friend who is a wonderful cook and she has her own catering business. God is using her gift to bless others. What these two women share in common is they love what they do.

I know someone who is very creative. She designs needlework patterns and sells them all over the world, and she loves what she does. Some of you reading this book love to work with your hands in creating artwork, scrapbooks, woodwork and the like. I could go on and on telling you about the different creative abilities of women I know, and I am sure if I could talk to you I would learn something wonderful about the things that you love to do. Women really are amazing!

Not all women love or even like to do the same things and that is okay. I don't enjoy cooking or sewing. I do those things for my family, but it is not a passion of mine. Although I don't really enjoy those two particular things my children never went to bed hungry, nor did they have to run around without any clothes on. It was my responsibility to see to their needs and I was happy to do that for them. The Jewish woman of her day was involved in making her families clothing as well as providing meals and a warm, cozy home to live in. We are no different. Although we have modern conveniences that they did not have our job hasn't really changed all the much.

Being a woman of virtue means doing these things with a willing heart. We do not view this part of our job as a wife and mother as a chore or some thankless task that we *have* to do. We do it because we love them and love to do this for them. We are to enjoy it, ladies! Now, the next time you have to clean the toilet in the children's bathroom try to think about doing that with joy! There is pride when you do something and you do it well. It may go unnoticed by your children and your husband, but it will not go unnoticed by God. Warren Wiersbe's Expository Outline on the Old Testament calls her a priceless woman. He writes:

"This priceless woman is a worker. Whether it be sewing or cooking, taking care of the children or assisting her husband in family business, she is faithfully doing her share. Note that she works willingly; it is not a matter of compulsion but compassion. She loves her husband and therefore seeks to please him." [14]

Okay, so you aren't Martha Stewart! Who cares? You have gifts that God will use to bring joy and delight into your families lives. Put those qualities to work. Pop on some rubber gloves, grab your iPod and dance around the house to your favorite music, cleaning as you go. The love you have for your family will show in even the simplest things like clean towels and folded clothes. God is more interested in our attitude than our abilities.

I enjoy watching HGTV and like most of you I often wonder if I could make my home look like those seen on TV. I am not an interior decorator and never will be. As I look around my house I am pleased; pleased that I have taken the time to make it feel like home. I don't need to compare my home with the home of anyone else, neither do you. <u>Magazines and</u> television shows have professional designers and those

14 Scripture quotations marked (NLT) are taken from the Holy Bible, New Living Translation, copyright 1996. Used by permission of Tyndale House Publishers, Inc., Wheaton, Illinois 60189. All rights reserved.

homes lack something very important. Family. These homes are not lived in they are just for show. One of your greatest treasures on earth is your family, and a home that has a little clutter is a home where love abounds. There will be time enough when the children are grown for picture perfect homes.

While we can set unrealistic expectations there are things we can do. You and I can do what Christ commanded us to do as unto the Lord. Our families should be at the top of our "love" list. When we stop and consider what we do to prepare for guests—clean and polish furniture, sweep the floors, clean the bathroom, vacuum the carpet, prepare a perfect meal and set an elegant table it would appear that somewhere our priorities have become a little mixed up. We need to do our everyday chores as if company were coming. After all God is to be our invited guest at every meal, right. So if we are going to invite God to be with us then shouldn't we work as though He were coming? This is in no way a suggestion that your home must be perfect, I raised two children and I know that I had many days when I just had to work around the clutter. Remember it is about attitude not ability. I cannot stress this enough, you are not going to do everything well, everyday, some days you are going to fall into bed completely exhausted and even frustrated. Okay, just say to yourself, "I am not Martha Stewart," and remember she does not do all the cooking and cleaning, she pays to have it done.

I need to stop here and tell you a funny story, because I raised two children, and I know that keeping and neat and tidy home is very challenging while you have children at home.

When my son was about ten years old I redecorated his room. I painted it the color he wanted, bought a new bedcover, and added a lot of sports paraphernalia on the walls. I thought if I gave him a room that he would be proud of (*I use the word proud loosely, what ten year old boy has a lot of pride in his room*) he would keep it clean. Wrong!

I came in from work one afternoon and went into his room. It was a complete disaster. I mean it looked like a tornado had ripped through it, really! There was so much stuff on the floor. I could barely walk without stepping on something. This was after I had asked him, no told him, for the tenth time to pick it up. Now I am mad!

I decided action was going to speak louder than words. I began to pick everything up off the floor, only I was not going to do the work he was supposed to do, so I piled everything single thing right in the middle of his bed. When he came in from playing outside the room was spotless, except for his bed, which now contained everything that had once been on the floor.

I told him that he would not be allowed to sleep in his bed until everything on it was in its proper place. (I *even took pictures of the room before I started... I was going to use it as leverage, for what I wasn't sure!*) He was mad, so he decided that he would just sleep on the floor. Of course, I finally convinced him, after some persuasion, that doing it my way was the best way. Parenting had its challenges. Keeping his room clean was never a priority to him. Never! It was a struggle until the day he left home. I laugh about it now but at the time it was frustrating. I know that you may face the same challenges, but it is possible to create an atmosphere of cooperation in your home, just use a little creativity. I even resigned from being a mother for a week, but that's another story.

Our virtuous woman delights in her work. That is a concept that we need not only in our homes but in our workplace as well. Because most American families live on two incomes your work may be *from* home, *outside* your home, or *both*. I applaud the young women today who can stay at home, at least until the children start school. There are many of you who work out of necessity, and that is okay.

Let's take another look at our verse again. Remember she works with her hands. Is it possible to apply this verse to the workplace? Of course. We have woman who are doctors, lawyers, truck drivers, steel workers, automakers, nurses, postal workers, soldiers, retail clerks, stock clerks, butchers, bakers and candlestick makers. The list goes on and on. The virtuous woman delights in her work, whatever her work is. Since we bare the name of Christ, we should conduct ourselves in a manner that reflects the character of Christ. Talking about co-workers behind their backs, or being caught up in office gossip does *not* reflect God's character. Why do we do this? Unfortunately, good, well-meaning, Christian women are often in the middle of these confrontations in the workplace adding their unwanted opinion along with everyone else. We should be holding each other up and not tearing each other down. Don't be part of bickering and backstabbing. We need to learn to walk away, literally, turn and walk away. Be intentional in taking a stand for what is right. Colossians 1:10 tells us to..."walk in a manner worthy of the Lord, to please *Him* in all respects, bearing fruit in every good work and increasing in the knowledge of God;"[15] We are to bear fruit, be a witness in the workplace.

When we think of a woman in scripture who seemed to display these qualities, Martha comes to my mind--not Martha Stewart, but Martha the sister of Lazarus. Why Martha, because Martha was a good hostess. She took pride in her home. One day when Martha knew that Jesus was coming to visit, she began to prepare for his arrival. She had spent the day cleaning and cooking, sound familiar. Reading between the lines of the scriptures, imagine with me what sort of activity was taking place in the home of Lazarus.

Martha had gotten up early that morning and gathered her baskets to take into the marketplace. She was going to pick out just the right fruits and vegetables for the meal. It was a very special day. Jesus, a friend of the family, was to be their guest. She picked out the fattest chicken and goose she could find and carried them back to her home to begin the preparations.

Martha was so busy that she hadn't even thought about her sister, Mary (who was nowhere to be found). She was far too excited about Jesus' coming to give much thought to anyone or anything else. She had to make sure that everything was just perfect.

Once she had decided on a menu and had the food preparations under way, it was time to clean house. Sweeping and dusting were a challenge since they had dirt floors and open windows. Nevertheless, she hummed a song as she worked. Martha would do her best to make sure that her guests would find her home comfortable. Fresh flowers were placed in vases and set around the house so their fragrance could be carried through the air by the breeze. The cushions were carried outside to air out, and the rugs were beaten to get as much of the dust from them as possible. Fresh linens were placed on the table along with the flowers.

Martha would return to her kitchen to put the finishing touches on the meal. She was doing what came natural for her. She certainly had the gift of hospitality, anyone who knew her would agree. Her virtuous character showed in the way in which she cared for her family and her guests. Things

15 ·

would have been fine had she not lost sight of that gift. But as the expected time of her guests arrival drew closer, it became very evident to her that she had done all the preparations without any help from Mary, who had not lifted so much as finger to help her. She became angry and sidetracked from her duties as she thought about Mary's untimely absence. "Where in the world is that girl?" she grumbled under her breath. "Here I have worked and slaved all day for this meal and I have not seen her anywhere." At that moment she heard voices. There was laughter and good-natured joking coming from just outside. Martha peered out the window just in time to see Jesus coming towards the house. Walking beside him were his disciples and Lazarus. When Martha heard Mary's voice among the others her anger was intensified. She had to pull herself together because she did not want Jesus to see her frustration.

Martha pulled the towel from her waist, wiped her hands on it and laid it aside. She laid it aside as she walked out to meet Jesus and his disciples. When her eyes met Mary's she gave her one of those "looks", the kind that says "You are in so much trouble." Mary shrugged her shoulders as if to say to "What's your problem?"

Jesus came close to Martha and hugged her, as a brother would his sister. Although she was smiling, He knew there was strife in her heart. Martha quickly dismissed the look she saw in his eyes and ushered them inside. She escorted Jesus into the room where they were to have their meal. Jesus reclined at the table. All of the guests there were listening intently to his words, including Mary.

While Martha was busy being hospitable, her sister was busy being the student. Martha brought out the meal and placed it on the table before them. Everyone voiced their delight and praised her for all her hard work. The meal was a success! Martha could not enjoy any of it because anger towards Mary consumed her thoughts. She quickly withdrew to the kitchen.

Jesus, noticing that Martha was not enjoying the guests at her table, rose and went into the kitchen to find her. Martha was standing next to the grinding mill. The tool that she had spent hours with grinding the meal to make the bread her guests were enjoying at this very moment, and tears filled her eyes. Approaching Martha Jesus asked, "Martha, what is it that is bothering you?" Martha looked up and brushed the tears away in defiance,

"Didn't you see my sister Mary sitting at the table eating a meal while I was in the kitchen slaving away? Don't you even care that I have done all the work by myself?" "Martha," Jesus spoke, touching her arm, "you have worried about too many things here today. There is really only one thing that is necessary and your sister Mary has chosen the right thing," As Jesus' words sank in, Martha's heart was broken; not because of Mary's actions, but because she had judged her wrongly.

"Put aside your work, Martha, and come sit awhile with us," Jesus told her. Feelings of guilt swept over her. She hadn't enjoyed the work of her hands; she hadn't even enjoyed the company of her guest, because she had been so angry with Mary. She dusted the flour from her clothes, and poured water into a basin to clean her hands, then followed Jesus into the next room.

As she followed Jesus into the next room, Mary and Lazarus were laughing, telling stories and enjoying the company of their friends. Martha smiled at them and moved to take a seat next to Mary on the floor. Mary touched Martha's hand and Martha's mood quickly lightened as she listened to her brother Lazarus, and Jesus laugh in good-natured fun. Although nothing had really changed, Martha alone had done all the work, suddenly she was laughing right along with them as if nothing else mattered. (You can read about Mary and Martha in the book of Luke, chapter ten.)

Some women identify more with Mary than with Martha. They would rather sit in a Bible Study, writing down everything that was being said, buying every book on the subject and memorizing all the scriptures. Others are more like Martha, they are the women who find great joy in making sure that your chair is comfortable, your plate is full, and your cup is never empty. God is so good in placing all the right parts in the body; not just our physical body but our spiritual body as well. Sometimes we get the "Martha" mentality and we don't take time to be a Mary. You see, Jesus wasn't unhappy with Martha for working so hard to make things pleasant. He was showing her that both she and Mary had priorities that were equally important, but that there comes a time when we need to sit at the feet of Jesus to learn, and forget about the "busy work" that we so often find ourselves doing.

Digging Deeper

1. Look up the word delight and write the definition below.

   _____

   _____

2. Read the following passages: Psalm 37:4, 40:8, 119:16, 47. Now write what we are to delight in.

   _____

   _____

3. Do you find that you are more like Martha or more like Mary.

   _____?

4. Does the work you do reflect a heart filled with delight, or a heart filled with despair? Write your answer here. _____

   _____

   Why or why not? _____

   _____

Pray this prayer:

Dear Heavenly Father help me to bring my will in line with Yours. Help me get my priorities in the right order. Let my family see that I love You first, my family second, and others last. Let my husband see in me a woman of virtue. When he looks at our children and his home let him know that he is loved, and may he find rest and peace within these walls. Amen.

Design # 5

"Setting Sail"

Proverbs 31:14 - She is like merchant ships; She brings her food from afar.[16]

I recently finished reading a book in which one of the main characters of the book was a merchant mariner. It was his job to bring goods from England, and to deliver them to the coastal cities of the United States. His ship carried items necessary for a comfortable life–food, fabric, furniture, just about everything that you could imagine. The goods were sold to local shop owners who would then sell them to the townspeople. That is commerce. It's the same today as it was 100 years ago; we still have merchant mariners who carry goods on massive ships and trade all over the world.

So what does that have to do with the Proverbs 31 woman? Just as merchant mariners will travel the globe to bring useful and sometimes exotic items to people everywhere, the virtuous woman searches diligently to find exactly the right things to bring home to her family regardless of the time or the effort it took to get them.

I can remember a time when my daughter was going to attend her high school prom. We lived in a small town, so we had to drive two hours to the nearest mall. When we arrived at our destination and started pricing dresses, I was in shock! I couldn't see paying that much money for a dress that she would only wear once. We shopped at several stores and finally

16 New American Standard

ended up in a department store that just happened to be having a sale, on prom dresses. There were racks and racks of dresses all marked down 50 to 75 %. She was given a budget and we were going to stick to it. Even though she wanted to have a dress that cost five times as much as the dresses on sale, she was willing to continue searching for a dress she would wear. After trying on what seemed like a thousand dresses we just could not find the right dress and we left disappointed. I knew that when the time came we would have a dress and she would look as beautiful as all the other girls, which she did, and within the budget! Although it would have been easier to just find a dress and pay full price it would have put our family finances under strain. We will make sacrifices over, and over again for our families, but those decisions need to be done carefully and prayerfully insuring that the decisions you make will in no way hurt your family's financial situation later. As my family's "merchant" I need to be willing to go the distance *and* be smart with my money. I love to find a great deal and I usually don't mind working a little harder at finding it.

At times, I wonder if God did actually create women to shop. I know very few women who do not like to shop. It's as if we were born for it– it's in our blood! *(Are you one of those women who will get up at 3:00 a.m. the day after Thanksgiving and do your Christmas shopping, come on admit it you know you are and you love it!)*? The trouble many women get into today is with the little "devil" called the credit card. It is so easy and convenient just to charge it. I know many women who have gotten into a lot of trouble with credit cards. Buying things when you do not have the money can lead to a lot of trouble at home.

Some time ago, I met a woman who appeared to be successful by the world's standards: she lived in a nice neighborhood, she and her husband both had great paying jobs, they drove nice cars and their children were involved in many extracurricular activities at school and at church. However, there was a problem. She had run up the balance on her credit cards, and she was trying to pay them down without her husband's knowledge and could not. As you can imagine, this led to a disaster when she finally had to ask her husband for help.

We must always be aware of the financial situations of our home. Whether you have your own checking account or share an account with your husband, make sure that you have a budget that fits your income/

bill situation. Whether or not you're the one who handles the finance of your home, you need to be involved in the decisions. Both spouses need to have a working knowledge of the bill payment schedule, etc. An involved partner who knows the account balances and the bills that are due can easily decide on non-necessary purchases. Little things can add up rather quickly if you are not careful. When you are looking for a special gift for your husband do you just shop at one place, and if they don't have what you are looking for, stop there, and just buy whatever you can find? No, you will go to the next place and the next place until you have purchased just what he wants.

The virtuous woman is a woman who puts the needs of her family above herself. Today it is harder and harder to put anyone above you. The world tells us to think of ourselves first. If we don't who will?

On the flip side of this, there are *many* women who will sacrifice their own *needs* so that their families have everything that they *want*. Notice I did not say *what they need*. They want to make sure that Jenny gets to take piano lessons, flute lessons, gymnastics, and cheerleading. They want her to go to the prom in the prettiest dress money can buy. In addition, let's not forget little Johnny either. We drive him to basketball practice, baseball practice, and guitar lessons. If that doesn't sound like your family maybe you live in a rural community and you might have to go to a rodeo or stock show to watch him show cattle, goats or lambs. Don't think that I am saying we should not do those things. I absolutely think you need to make sacrifices for your children. The challenge is making sure we keep those things in balance with our level of income. When Jenny needs a new flute and you need a new dryer, are you willing to make the old one work for a little while longer so that she gets her new flute? Sometimes we go overboard with our children to give them everything they want. That is not always in their best interest though. There may be times when the gifts you give need to come more from the heart than the wallet. These are often the gifts most cherished.

When it comes down to it, what we really want is to make our family happy, and we will go to great lengths to do it. Remember cherished memories don't always come with big price tags. We want to create memories with our families. We want them to have memories they will be able to look back on with fondness and love, remembering the things that we did for them when we were here on this earth.

The woman in verse 14 is one who makes sure that the cupboards are full, and who runs a well organized home. Organized? Huh Oh! That leaves me out of the "Top 31" you might say. Well, join the crowd. Some years ago, I read a book titled "Sidetracked Home Executives". It was a book written by two sisters who were terribly unorganized. Their book shared a system they came up with that got them organized. After reading the book, I decided that I would try their method and dove right in with the suggested "color coded card file". I made meal cards, planning my family's meals week by week. I logged every task, room by room, as suggested in the book. I categorized my chores on the color-coded index cards, and placed them in the file box under the appropriate day of the week, and month of the year. It was a tedious task cataloging everything from dusting, shampooing the carpets to cleaning toilets, but I did it! I was faithful to pull out my cards on the appropriate day and do the chore with enthusiasm and determination so I could get my house in order. I wish I could tell you 20 years later I am still working with my file box and the color-coded cards, but those cards have since been discarded. It is a tool that I no longer use. If you are a type A personality, one who is extremely organized, then this system might be of some value to you. If you are less than super-organized, you might find the book too much work. There is probably a book somewhere that will give you some great ideas.

Did you know that we not only have books to help us get organized, but you can actually hire a "professional organizer" to come into your home and help you get your life organized? The point is that you get organized, how you accomplish that will be up to you to decide. It is very important to have an orderly home, one that you are proud to have. When people stop by unexpectedly do they see a home lived in, yet orderly, or do they see a disaster area? Whether you live in a small home or a mansion, have to do all the housework yourself or hire it done, how you manage your home will say a lot about you.

You might live with a "neat freak" or you might live with a "pack rat". Whatever the family you have, you need to do your best to get your life balanced. Check your schedule. How does your day begin? Do you have to *pencil in* time with God? Are you too busy running the children here and there? In Barbara Fowler's Bible Study titled "Balancing at the Speed of Life", She writes: "As busy Christian women, many of us deal with this kind of daily commotion. Juggling schedules, children, job responsibilities, church and community commitments while trying to maintain some element of sanity can be overwhelming and discouraging."[17] We need to take time from the hectic schedules to spend time with our heavenly father. Getting recharged and refreshed helps to reduce the stress of daily living.

Let's look at a woman in the Bible who possesses the qualities of this Proverb 31 woman. We do not know her name but we find her story in Luke.

Luke sat down at his writing table, and dipped the quill of his pen in the ink well and began a letter to his friend. "I will write to Theophilus about what has taken place today. It will bring him much joy to hear how Jesus responded to those who sought to trip him up." Luke thought. He leaned forward pen in hand and began to write.

The sun was going down in the distance and Luke wanted to finish his letter to Theophilus before darkness filled the room. He had forgotten to buy more oil for the lamp today and he knew he would need to light the lamp on his writing table if he waited too long to finish the letter, and he had a lot to say to Theophilus.

"Dear Theophilus" Luke began, "Where do I begin with this story, there is so much to tell and I must get it all down correctly." Luke scratched his head thinking back on the week's events. How will I ever convey the right message to him?" he thought. Luke picked up the piece of parchment paper and stared at it for a long time before he wrote the next few lines.

"Today as Jesus was speaking to a large crowd of people in Capernaum. one of the Pharisees, named Simon invited Jesus to dine at his home. To our surprise, Jesus accepted the invitation. I am not sure why Simon wanted Jesus to dine with them." Luke stopped for a moment and thought back to the scene. Simon had walked right up to where Jesus was sitting with Luke and His disciples and asked Jesus to dine with him at his home that very evening. Jesus didn't hesitate before he answered. Of course, he would. There was no question at least not in the mind of Christ; he would go.

As Simon escorted Jesus down the road to his house, several others --Pharisees,

---

17 Fowlkes, Barbara, <u>Balancing at the Speed of Life</u>, (@ 2004 by Hensley Publishing,pg15.

most of them, met them. While it was customary for those who were with Jesus to be invited to dine as well, Luke remembered how uncomfortable he was going into the home of Simon, but since Simon was big on proper etiquette and had invited them, they all went. Each took their places at Simon's table along with the other guest (mostly Pharisees and lawyers).

Luke picked up his pen again and began to write, "Theophilus, I tell you Jesus remained calm as Simon began to question him about who He was and what He was doing. As the other guests joined in the conversation, it seemed obvious that they were looking for an opportunity to question, no badger, Jesus. As Jesus was reclining at the table a woman, (not just any woman, but the town prostitute) *came in... The words just began to flow as Luke recalled the scene that played out in his mind.*

"At first there was total shock. No one really knew what to do or say. What in the world, could she possibly be doing in Simon's home? No one there seemed to have invited her; in fact, they were appalled and angry at her very presence. But that didn't even seem to faze her in the least, because what she did next brought silence to the entire house." A smile crossed Luke's face as he pictured the scene.

"Here were all of these Pharisees and lawyers, in their regal attire, and in comes a woman, not just any woman a "sinner", into their midst. They were ready to take her out and stone her. This woman fell down right at Jesus' feet and began to weep, uncontrollably at first. She washed His feet with her tears and used her hair to dry them. Then she stopped and took out a vile of expensive perfume, and broke the seal. Theophilus, my friend, I wish you could have been here. She poured out the perfume on Jesus' feet." Luke was writing faster now as he thought about what he had witnessed.

"This seemed to anger those in the room, but the moment they began to speak out against her, Jesus stopped them. He did not seem angry. His voice was calm, yet His words cut deep into the heart of all those present. He told them, that as an invited guest, no one offered to wash his feet, yet this woman not only washed his feet she had anointed them with a costly perfume. I had never witnessed anything quite like this before. Jesus helped the woman to her feet and told her to go away from that place and sin no more. You could hear a pin drop at that very moment. No one could say a word." Luke set down his pen and leaned back in his chair and tears filled his eyes. The compassion Jesus had for this woman, a sinner, was unmistakable. The love this woman had for her Lord was priceless.

This story is one that makes our hearts rejoice and causes us to weep with her. Described only as a sinner seeking her Lord, this woman arrives on the scene, uninvited, with her alabaster box of very costly perfume. It was likely this perfume was one that was one commonly used in preparing a body for burial. We know this by studying the accounts of the Jesus' death; perfumes like this were used when they wrapped His body for burial. From this, we can see that this woman made a tremendous sacrifice in her offering to Jesus. We don't know her name, where she was from, or her living conditions, only that she was a sinner. I prefer to think of her as a sinner saved by grace and set free. Free to be a giver. Out of a heart was full of gratitude and love for the Lord; she gave Jesus the best she had to offer - her perfume in the alabaster box. She went to great lengths to give this gift to Jesus. She risked humiliation, rebuke and possibly even death for bursting in, uninvited. She gave little thought about herself but as totally focused on Jesus.

Within this small passage of scripture lies a big lesson for us. This virtuous woman shows us how to give *selflessly*. She was not concerned about the cost of her gift. She wanted Jesus to have the very best she could offer. Her desire was to be with Jesus and to give Him her best, and she did. We can too. When we seek to give God our best then our families will have the greatest gift they can have: a wife and a mother who loves the Lord with all her heart and seeks to please Him first. We will then be able to show them how much we love them, in the little, **and** the big things we do for them.

Digging Deeper:

1. Reflect on the last time you went to great lengths for someone in your family, what did you do? _____

    _____

    _____

2. Are you living within your means and keeping your spending under control? Yes _____ No _____

3. Are you balancing your time effectively, making sure that you spend time with the Lord each day.

    Yes_____ No_____ Sometimes_____

4. Make a list of some ways you can restore balance to your daily life.

    _____

    _____

    _____

    _____

PRAY THIS PRAYER:

"Lord, thank you for my family. Help me to keep my life in the proper balance especially when life gets hectic. Help me to love them but to love You more. I love them and I want them to have the best that I can offer. Help me to get recharged and refreshed. Keep my focus on You first, with an eternal perspective. .Help me to keep make my home a place of refuge for my family. Amen.

Design #6
"WHO NEEDS PAULA DEEN?"

Proverbs 31:15- She rises also while it is still night, And gives food to her household, And portions to her maidens.[18]

A few years ago I was at home recuperating from back surgery, and spent a lot of time to lying around watching cooking shows on the Food Network. I really enjoyed watching Paul Deen's cooking show. She has a lot of practical recipes and dishes that the average family would find appealing. Her show is not at all like some of the other shows on the food channel where the dishes are far too exotic for my family. Whether you're a basic "Betty" or "top chef", the ingredient that makes your cooking special is *you*. . What you do for your family out of love is what they will remember.

Our "virtuous" woman is one who gets up early in the morning, before the dawn, to prepare for her family's morning meal. We live in an age of modern conveniences like microwave or convection ovens, fast food, dine-in or carryout restaurants. We aren't too worried about having to get up with the chickens, (literally), to make breakfast for the family or to get the days meals prepared. We have food already prepared --frozen and ready to serve with the push of a button. I am thankful we have modern appliances that make life easier. There is something that I feel we have lost with this modern age. The *love* shown with every home-cooked meal and dish seems lost when your family is standing in line at McDonald's or KFC.

18

Advertisers try their best to represent their food as tasting homemade but the fact is that "fast" means just that– fast! There is no time to enjoy a meal, and no time to enjoy each other, because we are in a hurry. The restaurants are crowded, so we feel that we must eat and run. Even when we do have time to sit down for a meal with the family the kids are anxious to get up from the table, and your husband can't wait to watch the latest football game, golf match or just take a nap.

Think back a few years when you were younger. What do you remember most about your grandmother? Was it her cooking? Most of us remember the days of going to grandmas and having a home-cooked meal complete with six different vegetables, at least two meats, homemade bread and don't forget the fried apple pies. I miss those days. I have to admit that when it comes to cooking for my grandchildren, I don't spend hours in the kitchen slaving over a hot stove. They would rather go to the nearest fast food place and play on the indoor playground. Since times have changed, instead of spending all my time in the kitchen I have time to play with them. One of my granddaughters told her mother that she loved going to "Nana's" because "she plays with me". That meant far more to me than making sure that she knows I can cook. Time is the most valuable asset we have when it comes to our family—use it wisely and share it with those you love.

How do we equate the 21st century woman with the Proverbs 31 woman- in one word, love? It is love that makes your home just as warm as the one you remember from your childhood. Why do you think the "virtuous woman" got up so early in the morning and worked so hard to prepare food for her house and her servants? Love, that's why! She loved her family and it brought her great joy to see them enjoying the fruits of her labor.

When my granddaughters come to visit, we might make cupcakes, bake cookies or play with Barbie dolls. I am building memories and a relationship with then that I pray will be lasting and strong. I want them to know that they can count on their "Nana" to be there for them. I want them to remember the love that went into the things that I did for them. Later on when they are grown, I hope they will have fond memories or our time together. My heart is blessed each time my daughter calls me for a recipe that she enjoyed as a young girl. I like to think that she remembers the love that went into those meals and as she is spending time with her daughters, she is building the same relationship with them. All too soon, they will be grown and gone!

When my son moved away, I wanted him to have something that would remind him of home. He was moving 900 miles away, and would not be able to come home very often. Sunday lunch with the family would not be part of his normal routine. One year for Christmas, I decided not only to bake him some cookies, but also to put together a cookbook for him. I wrote down some of his favorite recipes with detailed instructions on how to prepare them, written in a way that even a man who does not know how to cook would understand. I thought that it would be a way for him to stay connected to his family. If you have recipes that your family enjoys you need to preserve them. They will be treasured long after you are gone.

The "virtuous" woman rises while it is still night to prepare food for her household. This reminds me of the many times that I have gotten up earlier than the rest of my family to prepare a holiday meal. I did this so that they would wake up to the smell of something wonderful cooking in the kitchen. I remember mornings at my grandparents' house. My grandmother would get up before everyone else and have biscuits baking in the oven. You could smell the bacon frying and the coffee brewing. It would cause us all to get out of bed, wipe the sleep from our eyes, and gather around the table together for breakfast. Some of the best family times have taken place around the table at any meal. It is a time when all the cares of the world seem less important.

By nature, I am not an early riser. In fact, you could say that I usually stay in bed until I absolutely *have* to get up. I know exactly how much time I need to get ready in the morning, and I cut it close most days. Like many women, I work outside the home. Now that my children are grown, and there is only Jim and I left, I don't get up and fix breakfast. I climb out of the bed and hit the floor running, so to speak, and out the door I go. I have tried to make it a habit to get up early, but never seem to make it last for more than a day or two. In my opinion, I believe God never intended for us to get up by an alarm clock; that is why He created the sun. I do not think we should have to get up before the sun comes up. It *ain't* natural! Only chickens get up that early. Nevertheless, when then need arises, I am more than willing to get up ahead of the sun to please my family.

Thankfully, God is the giver of day *and* night. No matter when you get up it is the act of love that your family sees and will remember. Some of us function better at night than we do during the day. You know the people I am talking about; the ones who you cannot even speak to until they have had their first cup of coffee. They have to be awake for several hours before they can do anything more than grunt at you. When it comes to staying up late at night, they have no problem; and while the rest of the world is crashing around 9:00 p.m. they are just getting started.

On the other hand, some people are fully awake the moment their feet hit the floor in the morning– fully engaged and ready for whatever the day has. I don't know about you, but I don't rely on coffee to wake me up. Just give me a few minutes in the shower and I am good to go for the next sixteen or seventeen hours. I don't "snap" or "grunt" at people until I have been up for hours. Normally, I can get up and get right to the things I need to do, and do it with a smile on my face.

When my children were at home, I would go in to wake them up in the morning singing a silly little song "Wake up, wake up you sleepy head. Get up, get up, and get out of bed." Unlike me, they were not happy people in the morning. They would pull the cover over their heads and beg me to stop singing. I have a fair singing voice, but at that early morning hour, they did not appreciate any sort of singing–good or bad!

It is our responsibility to create an atmosphere of joy in the home. Not only do we provide for their physical needs, the "virtuous" women is providing for the emotional and spiritual needs. In order to be prepared to provide for them in this way we, must have "true joy" to draw from. You cannot expect to give what you do not have. Christ is the source of the joy and it is vital that we make time to spend with Him, for in Him our joy is made complete. I like to read my Bible at night. I am more alert and focused at night than I am early in the morning. I love to be alone in my office at home. I can tell my husband that I am going out to my little hide-away to spend time alone with the Lord; he will leave me alone until I emerge from seclusion. I try to be very careful that I am not neglecting him or any of my other responsibilities. I am getting my spiritual battery recharged so that my devotion to him can be richer and fuller.

Even though I have my quiet time in the evening, I still need Jesus to go *before* me every day. I need to fill my mind with things that are pleasing to Him. I do not know if you work outside the home, but if you do maybe, you need a little extra help heading in the right direction every day. Some of the things I do to help me are posting scripture verses on my desk at work and listening to Christian music on my morning commute. If you are sitting in your car in the middle of the rush hour traffic turn on a Christian CD or your favorite Christian radio station for those 15-20 minutes on your way to work.

There is joy when we start our day walking with the Lord. Do you need more time? Are you mornings rushed and your day filled with a long list of things to do? Could you get up a little earlier? Try taking small steps to getting up a little earlier if you don't think you can manage 1-2 hours. Take small steps to getting an early jump on your day. What would an extra 15 minutes a day mean to you? What would an extra 30 or 60 minutes mean? What could you accomplish with that little bit of extra time each morning?

I know that we would all love to be more disciplined and I wish I could tell you that I have it all figured out and that is reason for writing this book. The fact of the matter is that I am just like you. I am a work in progress, just like you. I read books and I consider all the things that I need to do (and want to do) but I have failed many times. You will too. Don't give up. Keep working at it. You haven't failed until you stop trying. Philippians 1:6 tells us that God began a *good* work in you and that He will continue to work on you until He calls you home. This is my life's verse.

There are many benefits to getting up early. Take advantage of that time before the rest of the family gets up to gather your thoughts, plan your day, make breakfast, and focus on Christ. Spend time nourishing your spiritual body as well as your physical body.

I have a friend who is a great prayer warrior. She has spent countless hours interceding on behalf of others. Many times she wakes up early in the morning, sometimes 2 or 3 o'clock, and she will get up to pray. The Lord wakes her up to intercede for another person who is in need of prayer. Often she will wake up with someone on her mind, and she will get up and begin to pray for them, only to learn later of their specific need. She is not getting up to cook or clean. She is getting up for a much more important job than that– praying for a brother or sister in need. I love to hear her tell those stories of how God has used her in this way. She is so faithful. God knows that when he needs someone to carry a burden before the throne of heaven He can call on her. God wants more women like my friend. He wants women who would carry the torch in the wee hours of the morning for another soul who is burdened by a heavy load. Just like we find time to get up early in the morning to put a turkey in the oven so that our families will have a delicious meal to enjoy, we also need to be willing to get up in the early mornings for prayer. Praying for others seems like an easier task than praying for ourselves. We need to pray and ask God to grant us the wisdom needed for the day. Many times I have had a need for God to give me peace of mind and wisdom. There is no better time to get our day off to the best start possible than early in the morning. In my search of the scriptures to find a woman who I think depicts the Proverbs 31 woman I found Hannah. Hannah was a woman of prayer. We find Hannah in 1st Samuel.

Morning came quickly it seemed. Hannah rose as she did every day without the fulfilling blessing of motherhood. She could hear her husband Elkanah laughing with his children born to him by his other wife Peninnah. Hannah was a wife but not a mother. She had found favor with Elkanah and every year when he entered the temple for sacrifices, he gave to her a double portion because he loved her even though she had not born him a child.

Peninnah was jealous of Hannah and taunted her almost daily. "Hannah, why do you suppose the Lord has not seen fit to give you any children? What have you done to anger him so?"

Year after year, it was the same, Peninnah had given Elkanah more children and every year Hannah made the journey to the temple for sacrifice without a child. Hannah was so grieved that she could not eat and tears flowed, like a fountain. Elkanah hated to see her cry and questioned her repeatedly. "Why don't you eat something? Why are you troubled? Haven't I treated you better than ten sons, yet you cry and let Peninnah's words cut into your heart and cause you sorrow? I don't understand you, Hannah. So what if you have no children. I still love you."

Hannah heard his words but they could not ease the pain in her heart or the longing she had for a child. So, deep was her pain that as she made her way to the tabernacle she began to pray and weep uncontrollably. Eli, the priest in the tabernacle, was sitting on a chair by the doorpost of the tabernacle when he saw Hannah crying and mumbling to herself. He watched her closely, wondering what was causing her strange behavior. Hannah's arms were stretched towards Heaven and in her anguish, she beat her chest. It looked as though she was crying out to God but no sound was coming from her mouth.

Hannah was not even aware of Eli's presence as she began to pray. Her lips were moving, but Eli could not hear her speaking. Her inaudible words were intended only for the Lord. "Lord of Hosts, will you take notice of this your servant Hannah. Do not forget about me and please give me a son. I will give him in service to the Lord all the days of his life and never cut his hair, if you will but bless me, your maid servant." She barely spoke the words above a whisper. Eli could not hear what she was saying. He watched her moving back and forth. He noticed her lips moving like those of a mad woman and he became angry. He thought to himself, "This woman is drunk." He shook his head in disgust and thought, "How dare this woman desecrate the temple like this. Does she not know in whose presence she had found herself? Surely God would strike her down for such an abominable display."

Eli made his way towards the young woman and spoke, "How long are you going to stay drunk, put away your wine?"

Hannah quickly rose to her feet and wiped the tears from her eyes, "No, my Lord, I am not drunk; I am a woman with a broken heart. I have had nothing to drink, neither wine nor beer. I have been praying from the depths of my anguish and grief. Please do not think badly of me."

Eli was moved in his spirit for the young girl had spoken the truth, "Go in peace and may the Lord God of Israel grant the petition you have requested of Him. Hannah was moved by his words, and quickly left the temple gate. For the first time in many months, she was hungry and her joy had returned.

The next day Elkanah rose early and entered the temple again. When he returned home, he found Hannah waiting. Her sorrow was replaced with joy, and Elkanah's love for her burned within him. They shared an intimate evening together, and the Lord remembered her prayer. Hannah remembered the words of Eli, the priest, "May it be granted unto you, what you have asked of the Lord. Hannah believed God had used Eli to speak to her and she had reason to hope. A few weeks passed and Hannah knew that God had indeed heard her prayers. She was certain now that she was going to have a child. She also remembered her promise to the Lord and when she gave birth to her son, she named Samuel, because she had requested him from the Lord.

Today we find many parents dedicating their children to the Lord. They promise to raise them in the love and admonition of the Lord. I believe that we have Hannah to thank for the very first "baby dedication". If we had more mothers like Hannah, we would have more children like Samuel. It begins with prayer and continues all the days of our children's lives as we pray for them. The family that prays together stays together. Psalm 5:3 tells us: "In the morning, O LORD, You will hear my voice; in the morning I will order *my prayer* to You and *eagerly* watch".[19]

When we start our day with the Lord, we can eagerly wait upon the Lord for answers to prayers. In the mornings before the dust of the day has settled in on us we can praise the Lord with a grateful heart. Start your day on a happy note. Nothing will make the day better than knowing that the Lord is going before you. Elizabeth George in her book "Beautiful in God's Eyes" says that while we need our beauty rest it is more important to be getting the kind of beauty that God is talking about. Beauty on the inside may mean getting up early in the morning. You have heard the saying, early to bed and early to rise, makes a *woman* healthy and wise. There is truth to that. Getting a good night's sleep never hurt anyone and getting up early won't hurt you either.

DIGGING DEEPER:

1. How does prayer affect your day? _____
    _____

2. Read the following verses and match them with the phrase on the right about prayer.

2 Sam. 21:14	In the morning I will order my prayer
2 Chron. 7:12	We will devote ourselves to prayer
Ps. 5:3	God was moved by prayer
Acts 6:4	I have heard your prayer

---

19   New American Standard

3. Read Proverbs 20:13 - What advice is found in this verse?

_____

_____

_____

PRAY THIS PRAYER:

Lord I know that starting my day with you will bring peace and order into my life. Help me to make time each day for You. Help me to make my home a refuge for my family. Help me create a place where they too will find peace. Lord, we live in a fast-paced world. Help me to slow down, enjoy my family, and enjoy doing things with them and for them. Help them to see that I place a high priority on my time alone with you, whether day or night that they will respect my time alone with You. Help bring order into our confusion, joy into our sorrow and peace into our turmoil. Help me to create wonderful memories with and for my family. Amen.

Design #7

"Visionary"

Proverbs 31:16- She considers a field and buys it; from her profits she plants a vineyard.[20]

I

t is not a rare sight to see women in the corporate world. There are women who start their own companies, or work their way up the corporate ladder to become the chairperson or CEO of an organization. Women play an important role in today's society. From reading about the Proverbs 31 woman we find that God has used women in various capacities throughout history.

Do you know the story of Jeanne d'arc or Joan of Arc? Here was a young woman of vision. Literally. She claimed to have had visions from God beginning at the age of 12. In her vision, she was to help lead a faction of the French royal family called the "Orleanists" or "Armagnac's" against the English and the French faction called the "Burgundians." It was not until 1428 that Joan would receive an escort to speak to Charles of Ponthieu, later known as Charles VII, commander of the French Army and the last heir of the Valois dynasty, who had ruled France since 1328.

After receiving this audience with Charles, he was so impressed with her story that he provided her with a suit of armor made to fit her body, exactly, and a banner, which pictured the Lord holding the world with two angels at the sides. She was taken to an army where she began to reform the troops. She made them give up swearing and looting. She ran off the

20

prostitutes and made the men go to church. Word of her affect on the troops spread and men began to volunteer to serve in the French army to fight against England. Later we know that Joan was captured, tried, and convicted of treason against England, and put to death at the age of 19. Some years later, her conviction was overturned and the church elevated her to sainthood.

Today there are many examples of other women in history who have served their countries with greatness. There are also women in history who have served the Lord with the same vigor. I think about Mother Theresa and her work with the poverty-stricken in Calcutta, India, or Lottie Moon, who worked as a missionary in China in the late 1800's. Women have been and continue to be an important part of God's work.

Let's take another look our virtuous woman in verse 16. She considers the field and buys it. It is not just about buying and selling. It is about vision. The woman considered the field first. She gave a lot of thought to which field she would buy. She may have thought it would be a good school for orphans or, possibly, a new church in an area of town that had no church. It could have been a hospital for the unwanted of humanity. Whatever it was, she considered her purchase wisely. In vs. 24 we read that she was a businesswoman so with the profits she made from her investments and sales she planted a vineyard, whose fruit provided additional income for her. The scriptures do not tell us what she was going to do with the money, but this woman knew exactly what would help her family and her community. Not only does she consider how this purchase will serve as an investment, but also how this decision will affect her family.

In our hurry-up, busy world how many times do we stop to consider how our decisions will affect our families? Many times we act on impulse. We will buy cars or make other major purchases on an impulse, only to realize later what a negative impact our decision is having a on us financially. God expects us to consider our choices and to pray about them first.

Now I wish I could tell you that all of my decisions have been made that way. Wrong! Not at all. I am just like you. I am learning the same way that you are. Sometimes we have to make a mistake before we can learn from them. Have you ever done that? Have you ever made a decision that later you wish you could undo? Once the decision is made and the contract is signed, you have to live with it.

Several years ago, my husband and I decided to go "car shopping." I hadn't done any preliminary research on which car would be the best value, or what dealership offered the best prices. We just headed out one day and ended up at a car dealership about thirty miles from our home. On the lot there was a beautiful white Camero. I had never given one minute of thought until that moment about owning a "sports car" like this one. The car salesman came out as we were browsing and asked if we would like to "take her for a test drive." Of course, we jumped at the chance to take this car out for a "spin." The next thing I know I was driving home with this new car, very excited about my great deal, thinking that I had gotten a good investment. A couple of days passed and the salesman from the dealership called and said he had made a mistake. He said I was going to have to pay them an additional $700 for the car. We had a signed contract stating how much we had agreed to pay for the car. They were persistent, calling me every day for their money. After much discussion we returned the car and got my old car back. I have to admit it wasn't a pleasant experience. The lesson I learned was in my haste, I had *almost* purchased a car that was neither practical nor comfortable in the first place, on a whim. I thought I was going to have to live with my mistake. Fortunately, I did not. Too often, we do not learn from those lessons and end up making the same mistakes the next time the situation presents itself.

Of all the qualities of the "virtuous" woman this one I think is the hardest one for me to emulate and maybe for you too. When you make a decision like buying a car or a new home, have you and your husband weighed it out? I know there are a lot of you who do not work outside the home. Your husband's job has allowed you to stay at home. Maybe you have made those sacrifices so that you could be a stay-at- home wife and mother. This can also be a very important lesson on budget planning for you as well.

Let's say your husband gives you an allowance each week, or maybe he gives you his check. Now you must decide what you are going to do with the money. If you have an allowance each week, will you save that money until you have a need and then spend it? Will you save your money for that special something that you have been wanting? If you pay the bills, do you consider how you are going to make the money stretch from paycheck to paycheck? Are you frugal, or does the money burn a hole in your wallet until you have it spent?

I believe our "virtuous" woman was frugal. She wisely considered each purchase. When she had decided which field she was going to buy she already knew just what she was going to do with it, plant a vineyard.

We had a neighbor who lived across the street from us in a very nice home. When we were building our house, she and her husband came by and introduced themselves. She told us that they were planning to move. Using the profit they had made from the sale of their home they had bought some property, which they were going to subdivide. On the property was an old farmhouse that they renovated and lived in while they were developing the lots around them. After all the lots were sold, she considered her options. She bought another piece of land, and began to build houses on it. This was a wise choice because, while she was living in the old farmhouse, she was making an investment in her family's future that paid off. Her husband was cheering her on, just as I believe our "virtuous" woman's husband was doing.

Marriage is a partnership. Decisions should be made together. Decisions that involve household finances should be made together. The scriptures tell us that she considered it first, *before* she acted on it. I believe that once she had all the facts she presented it to her husband. We know that he was a leader in the community, and she trusted his counsel. She knew he would let her know whether or not her decision was a good one. Not only was his opinion important to her, but since God had designed her as his helpmate (Genesis 2:18), and she respected him as the head of the home (a position that God had given to her husband, (1 Corinthians 11:3), it was important to her that he was in agreement with her on this decision. Not all women have husbands like that, but this is God's plan for marriage. God *desires* that couples be one in all things. Like-minded. Do you see the relationship that God has with the church and why He refers to the church as his bride? When a husband and wife are like-minded, because they act as one, issues that require careful consideration are more easily resolved. Since Christ is the head of the church and the church is His bride, we are to have the mind of Christ (Philippians 2:5). We are to exhibit the same attitude that Jesus had.

Warren Weirsbe's *Expository Outline on the New Testament* states this: There is no joy or peace in pride and self-seeking. When we have the submissive mind that Christ had, then we *will have* the joy and peace that He alone can give.[21]

We should be working together in unity for the good of our families. There is joy, peace, and harmony within the families who practice this important principle.

Don't lose heart if you find that you do not possess all the qualities outlined in Proverbs 31. There is hope for you. There is hope for me. We all need a guideline for living. The woman described in this passage was not mentioned by name. We cannot pinpoint exactly who she is, where she lived, who her husband was, or what their standing in the community was. Even though we do not know her name, we know her character and we can learn from her even. I think that God intentionally did not tell us a name. The importance of this passage is not in "who she is" but "Who she served." She served the Lord by caring for her family and by submitting to the authority of God and her husband.

I want us to look at another woman in the Bible, but this time we are going to look at a woman who **did not** portray the qualities of the "virtuous" woman. Her name was Sapphira. We read about her in Acts chapter 5. At the time of this story, great things were happening in the church.

As word of Jesus' life and death spread throughout Israel, many men and women became followers of his teaching. Many of them came together (much like a family) and sold all of their possessions then gave the money to help further Christ's message of hope and salvation. They were all of one mind and spirit.

Joseph, better known as Barnabas by the disciples, sat with his quill in his hand looking over the document lying on the table before him. This property had been in his family for several generations. "What good is this to me? It is much better for me to sell the land and give the money to the work of the church

---

21 Strong, J. 1996. *The exhaustive concordance of the Bible: Showing every word of the test of the common English version of the canonical books, and every occurrence of each word in regular order.* (electronic ed.). Woodside Bible Fellowship.: Ontario

than to let this land sit barren and useless," he thought. He had not told Peter or the others that he was going to sell the land and give the profit to the church. He just knew that this was what God wanted him to do. There were others in their congregation who were selling property and giving it to the church, but Barnabas' land was sold for a generous amount.

The church was experiencing tremendous growth, and with that growth came many needs. Barnabas considered how he could help to meet some of those needs. As he looked over the paper, he dipped his quill into the ink and without hesitation signed his name. It was done. He took the money from the sale, left the room, and headed straight to the house where the apostles were. Once he arrived he noticed many others from their congregation were there, some giving gifts and others in need. Barnabas took the bag of money and quietly, without drawing any attention to himself, laid it at the feet of the apostles. "Here Peter, may Christ's name be praised throughout the land, and may no one here have need of anything that we cannot by the grace of our Lord provide." With that, he set the money down, turned and walked away. Barnabas did not wait for Peter to count the money. It was not important to him that Peter or anyone else know how much was in that bag. Word of his generosity spread quickly throughout the church as those who were present began to tell others about what they had witnessed.

A woman named Sapphira heard of Barnabas' generous gift to the church. Jealousy grew in her heart as she listened to the praises being given to him. "We also have land," she thought to herself. After hearing about Barnabas she ran to tell her husband, Ananias...

When she reached the place where he was, she found him alone, so she began to telling him what the congregation was saying. "Ananias, you will never believe what I heard today about Barnabas" she scoffed. Ananias was busy working on a chair that Sapphira had wanted him to repair. Since Sapphira's tone of voice was demanding his attention, he set down his file, pulled up another chair, and motioned for her to sit down.

Drawing a long breath Sapphira began to tell him everything concerning the sale of Barnabas' land. As Ananias listened, a plan began to form his in mind then he said, "We have land. Let's sell it and do the same thing. However, we won't give all of it to the church. Let's keep some of the profit for ourselves. We just won't tell anyone. Everyone will think highly of us, and we will be well- known in the city for our generosity."

Sapphira placed her hands on Ananias' and said, "I was thinking the very same thing. We are not well known. No one knows how much land we have, but after today everyone in the congregation will know who we are."

Over the next several days, Ananias and Sapphira worked diligently to sell their land and soon had a buyer. Now they had to make sure that Peter and the others saw what generous people they were. They discussed their plans and headed for the house where Peter and the other apostles were staying.

Peter made his way into the small room with the apostles. He had taken some time away from the others to pray. While he was praying, the Lord spoke to him about Ananias and Sapphira. He became sad when the Lord revealed to him the plan that was in their hearts.

Peter summoned Ananias into the room. With great excitement Ananias began to tell him about the land he had sold. There was nervousness in his voice as he spoke, "Peter, Sapphira and I had some land that we sold and we want to give **all** the money from the sale of the land to the church." Peter sighed a great sigh and his heart was grieved because he knew Ananias was lying.

"Why had he lied? He didn't have to give it all to the church. There were no rules stating you must give it all. He could have just given what he wanted. No one would have thought less of him for that," Peter thought to himself. He confronted Ananias with the truth, "Ananias, why has Satan filled your heart to lie to the Holy Spirit about holding back some of the money you made on the land? While it remained unsold, did it not remain your own? After it was sold, wasn't the money yours to do with as you wanted? Why is it that you have formed this lie in your heart? You have not lied to men but to God."

After hearing those words, Ananias fell to the ground, dead. All who were there to witness it were in shock. Some of the disciples covered his body, carried him out of the room and buried him.

Sapphira was waiting for her husband to return with the good news of how he had been praised for his generous gift. She had no idea what had taken place inside. She was playing the praises, they had expected to receive, over in her mind. "I bet that Peter is patting Ananias on the back for his generosity. Why I bet we get a special seat of honor in the church. I wonder what is taking them so long. Maybe they are discussing how to spend the money, giving Ananias and I credit for our gift.

Three hours pass and finally Peter sent for her. She hadn't expected Peter to call for her. "I wonder what he is going to say to me," she thought, "Ananias *must still be with them." She had no idea that he was dead. They had carried his body out the back door and had already buried him.*

When she entered the room, Peter asked her a simple question. "Tell me, did you get this price for the land?" He quoted a figure, and she knew it was the price she and Ananias had discussed telling Peter earlier.

Her response was, "yes." At that moment, she became a co-conspirator in the scheme to lie to Peter and to God. She could have set things straight and told him the truth, but she chose to be a party to the lie. Peter confronted her lie and informed her that she too would have to pay with her life and she fell dead.

This is not a pretty story on giving. We would have much rather learned about the goodness of their hearts and generosity, and to know that she worked with her husband to sell the land and, whether they gave it all or part to the Lord, that their hearts were turned towards God. What can we learn from Sapphira that will help us to be more like the woman in Proverbs?

Sapphira was a hypocrite, trying to make Peter and the others think she was something she was not. A "virtuous" woman is a woman of the highest moral character. Your words are to be spoken in honesty and truth. Would you cheat the Lord? If you would cheat the Lord, you would cheat them. Your family is looking to see how you respond to situations where honesty and integrity are concerned.

When you consider the "fields" of your life, what have those investments meant to your family? Were those choices made in haste costing your family food on the table or clothes on their backs? We are to devote our attention to the needs of our family. Sapphira was pretending to be someone she was not in order to gain approval. Don't try to be something that you are not. Your family loves you for the person you are, not the person you *think* you are. They see the real you. God sees the real you.

I want to share a personal story with you. In my early days as a young pastor's wife, I was attending the state convention for the very first time. We had little money. I *felt* as though I had nothing nice to wear. I wanted to make a good impression, but I could not afford to go out and buy anything new to wear. I decided that I would just make something to wear. I was not a seamstress, in fact, I really hated sewing, but there was a wonderful lady in our church who helped me. We worked hard on "our" project, and when it was finished I was proud of my accomplishment. When I arrived at the convention I looked around and suddenly felt very "out-of-place". The women were all dressed in suits and expensive dresses. To make matters worse, a woman in the restroom asked me if I was pregnant. Now I really felt out of place! I wanted to hide from everyone there. I was so embarrassed and very self-conscious. That night while at my sister-in-laws house I told her about the incident. She went through her closet and pulled out a dress that was much more "fashionable" than the one I had brought and loaned to it me to wear. We bought a cheap pair of black high-heels and I wore her outfit the next day. I felt like I fit in with the rest of the crowd and I decided that I would never look out of place again. That was not exactly what God wanted me to learn from my experience.

Have you seen the movie "Gone With the Wind", remember spoiled little Scarlet's scene when she had lost everything and she vowed she would "never be hungry again." I was acting just like that when I vowed I would never look out of place. In truth, God was not interested in what I looked like on the outside. He was and *is* far more concerned with what I look like on the inside, the attitude of my heart. It really does not matter whether I buy a dress at Macy's if what is on the outside is nothing more than a facade. We need to devote ourselves to becoming a pearl of great price, a treasure to God. That, girlfriends, should be the desire of our hearts. Our motives should not be about self-recognition. It is about service. Serving our families and serving God. Sapphira was playing a part. Her outside did not match her inside, and God saw right through it. He sees through ours as well.

It is great to dream. We all have gifts and talents that God has given us. We need to look deep within ourselves and find out how we can best serve God with what he has equipped us to do. You go girl! Shine from the inside out!

Digging Deeper

1. What sort of dreams do you have for your family?

   _____

   _____

2. How do your decisions affect your family?

   _____

   _____

3. Read 1 Cor. 11:3, write it out here: _____

   _____

4. What does this verse tell you about the position God has given your husband? _____

5. How can you best serve God with your gifts and talents?

   _____

Pray this prayer:

Lord, I know that you have given me vision. I pray that my vision is in line with yours. Help me Lord to seek you in all my decisions and to make sure that my choices have a lasting joyful affect on my family. Thank you, Lord, for the wisdom of my husband and help me to seek his advice before I act. Lord, help me always to be honest and trustworthy in all my dealings in and outside of the church and with my family. Most of all let them see that I have the mind of Christ and the beauty of the Proverbs 31 woman.

Design #8

"LET'S GET TO WORK"

Proverbs 31:17 - First thing in the morning, she dresses for work, rolls up her sleeves, eager to get started.[22]

There are days when I wake up that I am anything but "eager" to get to work. I know that what faces me may not be as pleasant as I would like it to be. Maybe you feel the same way. Perhaps you have a difficult boss or a co-worker who tries to make things as hard on you as possible. Most of us have had to deal with those types of people. They live to be miserable and they want to make us miserable as well.

The picture here in verse 17 is quite different from what may be the normal routine in our life. We see here that when she gets up in the morning, she gets dressed for work, whether it is work outside the home or work inside the home, She sets her mind on the tasks before her and with eagerness gets her job started. In some ways, I am like that. The first thing I do every morning when I get up is get my shower, which helps me wake up. I fix my hair, put on my makeup, and get dressed, and then I am ready for whatever I need to do. I am not saying that I have to have my makeup on before I can clean the toilets. However, I am dressed and ready for the activities of the day whatever they may be.

I think that it is important for us to look forward to doing things for our families, and that includes rolling up our sleeves and getting down to

---

22 Peterson, Eugene H.: *The Message: The Bible in Contemporary Language.* Colorado Springs, Colo. : NavPress, 2002

business. We all know women who do not work outside the home. If you went to their home you would find total chaos: dirty clothes in the floor, dirty dishes in the sink, newspapers and magazines everywhere, and no order to anything. Other women make their homes look like they have the HGTV design teams come in daily to clean and decorate. Nothing is out of place. Those are two extremes, and there is something we can learn from both of these types of woman.

There was a television series on TV where two women swapped families for two weeks. The producers of the show would find two women who seemed to be extreme opposites from each other. They move into each other's home for this two-week period. The first week they had to live by the existing rules of the house, whatever that may be. In each of the homes there were extremes. One home had no rules while the other home had strict rules. During the second week, they could change the rules and their "new" family had to do whatever the "new" wife wanted. I cannot imagine living with another family other than my own for two weeks nor would I want another woman living with my family for two weeks.

I only saw the show a few times and on one of the episodes one wife and mother was a neat freak. She cleaned her house top to bottom every day. I mean top to bottom. She mopped and dusted every day. She vacuumed and did laundry every day. She cleaned the baseboards and around the toilets on her hands and knees every day. She spent hours and hours out of her day cleaning. Her family was expected to do the same. Mealtime was just as structured. They ate only healthy nutritious meals. No "junk" food. The children were not allowed to have a pet. The other wife and mother had NO rules. They lived to play and little, if any, work ethic. They rarely took bathes, washed their clothes or even attempted to clean house. They had not one pet but twenty pets of all kinds. The children were allowed to do as they pleased. There was no structure. They ate whatever they wanted. If they did not want to go to school, no problem, they did not have to go. These two families could not be more opposite of the other.

How do you think things went for those two weeks? Just as you would expect. Disastrous. Right! While there were rules, or lack thereof, for each family there was something that they could learn from one another. The rigid wife learned that her family could enjoy and take care of a pet without disrupting the entire order of the home. She also learned that she needed to loosen up a little. While the very "laid back" wife learned that her home could use order. She learned that she could live with a clean kitchen and bathroom. Having some order was not that bad after all. The children learned some things as well. They learned that people could be different and still co-exist.

"So what does this have to do with our virtuous woman?" I am glad you asked. She has balance and order to her life. She knows these are necessary. She also delights in it. She accepts the challenge with eagerness. She is not too rigid nor is she too laid back. Her home and her work are a source of pride for her. She is not puffed up with pride but she is proud of her home and the work she has done there.

Many of you may have someone who comes in once or twice a week to clean house for you because you hate housework, you do not have much time for it, or you just like the freedom of not having to do it. I have never had a housekeeper (*not that I would not have loved to*). If there is work to be done, I do it. I must tell you that since the children are gone the housework is much easier and my husband is a great helper. As I told you before, he does all the laundry. I take a lot of pride in my home. I love to see it clean and orderly. I want my home to be ready for company at anytime. I want people to feel free to drop in. I don't want to worry that the house is a mess. Most days I try to make sure that the bed is made before I leave home. I don't like to leave dishes in the sink all day. That may seem silly, given the fact that there are going to be more dirty dishes after supper, but I just like leaving my home knowing those things are done. I also try to make sure before I go to bed that all the dirty dishes are in the dishwasher. I don't like clutter, (especially newspapers), but I am not a "neat freak" I believe that a home doesn't have to be a show place. It needs to have a *homey* lived in feel to it. Not like some homes where you are afraid to sit on the furniture. Have you been in a home like that?

The New Living Translation tells us; *She is energetic and strong, a hard worker.* I like to think that not only is she concerned about the work at home but also she is also concerned with being energetic and physically fit. She has taken care of her fitness, and her energy level is up to the task. Women wear many hats: wife, mother, nurse, cook, housekeeper, coach, teacher and bus driver, just to name a few. The fact that we do all of these things requires us to have the energy and strength necessary to get the job done. This woman is the $6-million-dollar woman. She is a hard worker. She can keep up with the kids, her husband, manage a house, play 18 holes of golf and take in a game of tennis all before supper. She is a superwoman.

Recently I had to make a decision about my own physical fitness. I am not one who really looks forward to working out, primarily because I don't like to do it alone and I need motivation, *as if looking in the mirror isn't motivation enough.* I have tried many different exercise routines. I own exercise videos and have purchased numerous different pieces of exercise equipment, (all of which have gathered more dust that anything.) My intentions are good, but my desire to be fit is not matched with enthusiasm. Every year I decide I am going to get in shape. I signed up one fall, late in the semester, for a "Body Pump" class. It is a free weight-lifting class set to upbeat music. I decided to join on the assumption that I would have a "partner" to keep me motivated, not so, my partner lasted only two sessions and left me to attend class alone. I was determined to see it through. I have tried many different methods of staying in shape. I joined the gym, bought exercise DVD's, joined a running clinic and even tried the latest craze, Zumba. I need to be energetic and strong so that I can continue to work hard. The older I get the harder that is. It requires a lot more motivation and determination. I admire woman in their senior years that look and feel great. I want to be like that too. I want my "golden years" to be just that "golden." I don't want to be plagued with aches and pains, having no energy to get out of bed and do anything or enjoy my life after retirement. I have given all of those methods an honest attempt, unfortunately I have not stayed with any of them long term. Once again, I have to make a decision to get in shape. That is okay because I am not giving up. I will find something I really enjoy doing and stick with it. The whole idea is to keep trying.

There is a woman mentioned in the Bible by the name of Priscilla and we find her story in the book of Acts. Little is known about her, but what we do know is that she and her husband were tent makers and followers of Christ.

Paul, an apostle of Jesus Christ, had just finished preaching the gospel in Athens when he made his way to Corinth. There he would find his friends, Priscilla and Aquila, and he would spend some time with them. The past few weeks had been difficult for Paul and he was looking forward seeing them again. Paul knew that Priscilla and Aquila would be eager to hear of this work in Athens.

Priscilla and Aquila were tent makers, who had left Italy because Claudius, the fourth Emperor of Rome, had forced all the Jews out of Rome. They had come to know Paul when they lived in Rome and became followers of Christ after Paul's conversion experience on the road to Damascus.

"Aquila, how long has it been since we have seen our friend Paul?" Priscilla asked as she mended a hole in one of the tents a local merchant had brought to them. Aquila laid down the piece of leather that he was examining and answered her.

"I'm not sure, but it has been quite some time. The last letter we received from him came from Athens, which is not too far from here. If I know Paul, he won't pass by this close without stopping in for a home-cooked meal."

Priscilla put down her needle, placed both hands on her hips, and laughingly replied, "I certainly hope not. I won't forgive him if he does. Besides, I want him to meet some of the families we have written to him about and hear about his work in Athens went as well.

"Don't worry; I'm sure we will hear from him soon. His last letter said he would be leaving Athens very soon, because his work there was complete. He has started a new church to carry on the work of Christ there."

"I think it would be a good idea to let everyone know that we will be expecting Paul soon. I'm sure they will want to make preparations to be here. They've heard us talk about Paul so much I know they won't want to miss an opportunity to meet him and hear him preach."

"I think that is a good idea but don't you think you should to wait until Paul arrives? I would hate for you to get their hopes up only to be disappointed when Paul does not come as you expect."

"He wouldn't dream of not coming by here. We are like family," and with that Priscilla headed out the door. "I will be back soon. I want to get the word out that Paul is coming."

Aquila knew better than to try to stop her, she was probably right anyway. Paul would not pass through Corinth or even close by without stopping to stay with them for a few days. He picked up the piece of leather he was working and shook his head as he continued with his work.

Paul was only a few short miles from Corinth and was excited about his *visit. He was eager to wash some of the dust from his weary feet, and have some of Priscilla's cooking. He had traveled a long distance on this missionary journey and he was tired and hot. All he could think about was sitting down and relaxing with old friends. He had no idea that Priscilla was planning for him to speak to the church at Corinth. A smile crossed his face when he thought about seeing them again. They were dear friends who loved the Lord and he was sure that they would welcome him with open arms.*

Priscilla and Aquila were outside working on a tent. They were almost finished with it when Aquila noticed someone coming up the road. He stopped for a moment trying hard to see who it was. From that distance, he could not really tell who it was but there was something familiar about this person. Priscilla was standing behind the tent and could not see anyone coming towards them. Suddenly Aquila, recognizing the man coming up the road to be Paul, dropped his end of the tent and took off running towards him. The tent fell to the ground and Priscilla yelled out to Aquila, "Aquila, what are you doing?" It was not until that moment that she realized Aquila was not even standing there anymore; in fact, he was already halfway down the road. She let go of her end of the tent, no need to hang on to it now that Aquila had left her standing there. "Who was he running towards?" she thought.

*Aquila reached Paul and both men embraced each other and began to laugh and talk simultaneously. Each one slapping the other on the back, taking turns laughing and talking as they walked back toward Priscilla. Priscilla continued to stare at them in wonder. She still did not recognize Paul. She could not see his face. Then suddenly she knew it **was** Paul and she ran down the road towards the pair. Paul looked away from Aquila to see Priscilla running towards them and he patted Aquila on the shoulder, and motioned to his wife. Aquila nodded and Paul ran to greet her. As he reached Priscilla, he extended his hands to her and she placed her hands in his. Then spontaneously she threw her arms around him and gave him a hug. "We don't stand on formalities here, Paul, and you know it," she laughed as she released him. Paul stepped back and gave a hearty "Amen, Sister!" as Aquila walked up to join them.*

The three of them, Priscilla on one side of Paul and Aquila on the other, walked arm in arm towards the house laughing and talking.

Night fell as the three friends finished their meal. Aquila rose from the table to light the lamps as Priscilla and Paul were discussing his mission in Athens.

"Paul, we heard good news about the work in Athens," Priscilla said as she cleared the plates from the table. Paul leaned back on the pillows and began to tell them about his last sermon in Athens before he left.

"They are a complex group of people, Priscilla, they serve many gods there and if was difficult to break through their superstitions about God. They have erected idols to every god they can think of; they even have a monument to an "unknown" god. I used that particular monument to tell them about the one true God, because He is the one they "do not know." Many received Christ but many more of them were mocking and laughing when we told them of Christ's resurrection."

Priscilla's heart was broken for those who had rejected the gospel, but she quickly turned the conversation to their own work in Corinth. Her tone of voice was upbeat as she told Paul about the men and women in Corinth who were coming to their home each week to learn more about the work of the Lord.

"Paul, we have invited the people of our congregation to come to our home tomorrow night to meet you. We have told them about you and the message you are delivering. They want hear a message of hope. They are eager to work, but they need to hear that their efforts are not in vain. They have heard the stories of how difficult the work has been."

"I would love the opportunity. I will be at the Synagogue on the Sabbath teaching both the Jews and the Greeks and I would welcome their prayers for my message that day."

Paul remained with them for a year and a half

Priscilla and Aquila were also leaders in the church and held church in their home. Priscilla's name is not mentioned in scripture apart from her husband, Aquila. They were partners in ministry and worked with Paul after their conversion to spread the gospel. Because Priscilla was in business with her husband as a tentmaker, a predominately-male occupation, she must have been a very diligent worker and a competent businesswoman. She was also a committed Christian. She worked tirelessly alongside her husband and with Paul to teach young Jewish men like Apollos, who later would become a tremendous preacher and a very influential minister. Paul must have been very fond of this couple. He spent a great deal of time with them, and they got more than an "honorable mention" in scripture. Their love of Christ captured the heart and attention of Paul as he traveled about spreading the gospel. When Priscilla was laboring for the Lord, she was doing so with energy and enthusiasm.

Whether we work for someone outside the home or for our families, our labor will not go unnoticed when we work with energy and enthusiasm. Your family will notice and those you work with will notice. They cannot help but notice. Your energy and your enthusiasm will be infectious. People will want to be around you. They will see your good works and they will know that you are a woman who loves the Lord. He will receive the glory.

Digging Deeper

1. How would you describe yourself, are you an energetic or less than enthusiastic worker? *(Remember to be honest in your answers no one else is going to see them)*

   _____

2. What are some things that you do to stay motivated? *(I like to listen to music; in fact, I am listening right now as I write.)* _____

   _____

3. Read Proverbs 16:3 and fill in the blanks – Commit your _____ to the Lord and your _____ will be established.

4. Read Psalm 128:2. What does the Psalmist say is the result of fruits of your labor?

   _____

PRAY THIS PRAYER:

Lord help me to rise in the morning and get out of bed ready to meet the challenges of the day with energy and enthusiasm. Give me the strength and desire to make my home presentable each day. Lord, your desire is for me to be a helpmate to my husband and to be seen as a woman who loves You so that You will be glorified in all I do. Walk before me and show me the way to live that brings honor and glory to You. Amen.

Design #9

"Midnight Madness"

**Proverbs 31:18 - She senses that her gain is good;
her lamp does not go out at night.**[23]

I love a good bargain. I enjoy shopping when there is a 50 or 75% sale going on. It makes me feel like I have been a good steward with my money when I know that I have paid less than full price for something. In fact only on rare occasions do I even look on any rack that doesn't have a sale sign on it. I just hate to pay full price for things. We have stores in our town that are always having a sale. I have to ask myself is it really a sale or is the mark up so much that they are still making a nice profit when I buy it "on sale?"

Our "virtuous" woman is a woman who loves a good bargain. She will travel all over town just to save money. Besides being thrifty, there is another side of this woman that we need to see here. She knows the value of her work, and will work late into the night. (The Message Bible reads this way. *She senses the worth of her work, is in no hurry to call it quits for the day.*) How many women do you know who feel that way about their work?

Just the other day I was cleaning my bathroom— not at all a glamorous job. I do not really enjoy the job of cleaning the bathroom. However, once I rolled up my sleeves, put on my rubber gloves, and dove in, I was committed to seeing the task to completion. The job normally would have taken just a few minutes to do, but I wanted my shower squeaky clean as

23

well as the rest of the bathroom. So 45 minutes later it was finished. No one else cared anything about how long I spent cleaning the bathroom. It was not important to my neighbors or my friends that my bathroom was spotless. It was important to me. I knew I had done a good job and was pleased that I had taken the time to tackle it.

Now there are other jobs more important in life than cleaning the bathroom. We all have jobs to do. Your job may be to care for small children or elderly parents. Your job may be to read to sick children in the hospital or write letters to war-weary soldiers. You may have a job outside the home that takes up a lot of your time. Whatever your tasks are, consider how you perform those tasks and whether or not you are willing to work late to get the job done. Once again, our "virtuous" woman is a woman who has gained a reputation of being energetic. She is not only treasured by her husband (Proverbs 31:10) but, she is also a wonderful businesswoman (Proverbs 31:16), and she is adored by her children (Proverbs 31:28). In the midst all of that she is still able to look upon her work with a sense of pride.

There have been many times in my life in which I wanted to do something important. I felt that my own sense of self-worth depended on what I could accomplish with my life. I began working in the medical profession just after the birth of my first child. I was attending a Bible study lead by Kay Arthur at the Reach Out Ranch in Chattanooga, Tennessee where I was living at the time. While I was there, she told about a doctor who was looking for someone to work in his office as a receptionist. We had just moved to town, and I knew no one. I was eager to apply for this job. I knew that I was going to need to find a job, and this opportunity was very appealing, so I called the office and set up an interview. I asked my neighbor across the street if she would watch my daughter for me while I went to my interview. She agreed. Just after I dropped Breanna off at my neighbors, I ran back inside my house to get something I had forgotten. I locked the door to the house and ran to the car. You guessed it! I had locked myself out of the house, and my car keys were inside. I lived in a two-story house and I had no way to get in. I was panic-stricken. What was I going to do? I was going to be late for my interview. I called the doctor's office and explained what happened. I told them I would be there as quickly as I could. My husband was working out of town, and he had the only other set of keys. I was frantically trying to break into my own home when my neighbor's husband came home, and helped me get in. I arrived at my interview an hour late, and I was so flustered that when I told doctor what happened, I sounded like a rambling idiot. Much to my surprise, I got the job.

If God has blessed you with a job in these trying, economic times praise Him for that. If you find yourself without at job, keep praying, God knows your needs.

The virtuous woman is also proud of her work. She is not a lazy person either. She stays with the job until it is finished. Just like cleaning my bathroom, (as much as I would have rather done something else) I stayed with it until it was finished. She has a household to run. She is the mistress of the estate and with that comes responsibilities. She isn't sitting around and letting others wait on her, she is busy seeing to it that the home is taken care of properly. While I do not live on an estate, the running of the household has been my responsibility.

What sort of attitude do you think the virtuous woman had about her job? Did she tackle those tasks with grumbling or complaining, or did she do it with enthusiasm and joy? I can hear some on you saying, "Well she didn't have to work with those people I work with, or she obviously didn't have a family like mine." There were days when I go into work and heard nothing but grumbling and complaining. Sometimes the moment I walked through the door until the end of the day there was a constant rumbling of discontentment in the workplace. I placed a verse of scripture over the area I worked to remind me that God wanted more from me. The scripture is found in Philippians chapter two verses 14 and 15. *Do all things without grumbling or disputing; so that you will prove yourselves to be blameless and innocent, children of God above reproach in the midst of a crooked and perverse generation, among whom you appear as lights in the world,*[24]

We can get caught up in the world's grumbling and complaining, but God calls us to be different. We are to be blameless and innocent. The word *blameless* comes from the Greek word (amemptos) or un-blamable, faultless and free from defect and the word innocent, *(akeraios)* means pure

---

24 Strong, J. 1996. *The exhaustive concordance of the Bible: Showing every word of the test of the common English version of the canonical books, and every occurrence of each word in regular order.* (electronic ed.). Woodside Bible Fellowship.: Ontario

and simple.[25] We are to be faultless, pure, and simple. I love that. We use that phrase "pure and simple" when we are stating facts. God says that in the crooked world in which we live, we are to be found without fault, pure and simple. I realize that this is a rare thing in the world today, but it is to be our desire. If you are like me, you need those reminders as well. I'm not perfect, but as a member of the body of Christ that I am to conduct myself in a manner that speaks light to the dark world.

Our attitude towards our work should be free from the grumbling and complaining that often accompanies our job. No one likes sticking her hands in the toilet, but someone has to do it, right? (So do it with joy.) This can be said of a great many things. Whether your job is smelly, literally or figuratively, do it with joy! Be willing to go the extra mile if necessary and don't complain about it. God rewards those who run the race and finish the course.

The virtuous woman is an amazing woman. She is full of many great attributes that elude most of us. We aren't perfect. We are being **made** perfect. We are being formed and fashioned into the image of Christ. Don't think that you will achieve perfection. Focus on what does God want from you.

His desire is best described in Colossians 3 verse 23: *Work hard and cheerfully at whatever you do, as though you were working for the Lord rather than for people.*[26] We are to do just that. God's word speaks to our hearts and transforms our thoughts and actions. In any job, whether we work at home or outside the home, we can have a joyful attitude because we are working for the Lord. What others see in us, may in fact, be all that they have ever seen of Jesus. There will be days of great trial. Days when the dirty laundry is piled higher than the washing machine and your child's room looks like hurricane Katrina hit it.

You may have trouble finding joy in those tasks, but take heart sister; you are not alone. There is rest for the weary. You are among the thousands of women in the world who face the same challenges every day that you do.

---

25 Strong, J. 1996. *The exhaustive concordance of the Bible: Showing every word of the test of the common English version of the canonical books, and every occurrence of each word in regular order.* (electronic ed.). Woodside Bible Fellowship.: Ontario

26 Scripture quotations are taken from the Holy Bible, New Living Translation, copyright 1996. Used by permission of Tyndale House Publishers, Inc., Wheaton, Illinois 60189. All rights reserved.

Do you find that when all is quiet at home and evening has come–the children are in bed, the laundry is folded, and the dishes are done that you still have energy to get something else accomplished? Perhaps that is the time you are your most creative. I believe God has blessed us with this energy level so that in addition to managing a home we can still find time to be creative. If you are like most women, you probably have projects or hobbies that you love to do but never seem to find the time to, actually, do them. Maybe you could steal away for a few minutes late in the evening, after your work is complete, to do some of those things.

God has a job for you to do. Whether it is big or small, He needs you. Maybe God has called you to be a prayer warrior. In the wee hours of the mornings, perhaps you have been on your knees before the throne of heaven interceding for your brothers and sisters. God bless you. You will be rewarded for those hours you gave. Has God called you to teach a Bible study but the only time you have to study is in the evening. Maybe God is waiting for you to meet him after the day's work is done in the evening hours.

In the book of Acts, we find another "virtuous" woman... She is a woman we know very little about, but the scripture describers her as *joyful*. Her name is Rhoda.

It was late when Mary, John Marks' mother, had opened her home for a special prayer meeting. Rhoda, Mary's trusted servant, had welcomed Mary's guests into the home and did her best to make them feel welcome.

Rhoda had been present on numerous occasions when followers of Jesus had come into Mary's home. She too was a believer. Mary had shared the gospel with her quite some time ago. Although she had never met Jesus in person, she loved Him just as much as anyone who had actually walked and talked with Him did. She was not only a trusted servant to Mary, she was a servant of Jesus Christ.

Word came to them that Peter had been taken prisoner. They were all there for a specific reason––to pray for the release of their friend Peter. She had heard Peter preach many times. Tonight she would stay with the quests and pray for her friend, and brother in Christ, Peter.

With heavy hearts, they prayed earnestly for Peter, as they feared for his life. Many believers who served Christ had paid with their lives for doing so.

Peter loved Christ and was completely devoted to furthering the Kingdom of God, no matter what the cost.

Rhoda provided drink and nourishment for Mary's guests at her request. She never once thought about retiring to her room and leaving Mary to take care of them. She wanted to stay up and pray with them. It seemed as though they had been praying for hours, but they were determined to continue to pray through the night. Rhoda sat closest to the door of Mary's home waiting for the arrival of other guests who might join them.

Suddenly there was a knock at the door. No one moved and they continued in prayer. Rhoda rose from her position near the door and moved quietly to see who was joining them at this late hour.

*When she opened the door, Peter was standing there. Shock overcame her and before she realized what she had done, she closed the door. It could not be Peter; he was in prison. After all, that was the reason they were there, to pray for Peter. She must have been dreaming, wishing it to be him. No, it could not be a dream; she thought and quickly opened the door again. It **was** him! It really was Peter! So much joy overcame her that she left Peter standing at the door, ran back to where the guests were praying, and burst out, "He is here, Peter is here!"*

Rhoda's interruption in the middle of their prayer annoyed all those who were there. They thought she was delirious. They all knew Peter was in prison. It was impossible that the person standing at the door was actually Peter. One of the men stood up and moved towards Rhoda with his finger pressed against his lips. "Shhhh, can't you see were are praying", he whispered.

"But---" and before she could finish, there stood Peter in their midst, laughing. The thought of how absurd it must be for them to see him standing among them delighted him so that he could not contain himself.

"See, I told you it was Peter," Rhoda shouted. At that moment, everyone stood to their feet amazed that God had truly answered their prayers.

It was late into the night, and Rhoda could have grumbled, complained and muttered under her breath, "who in the world would be knocking at this late hour?" Had she not been a follower of Christ, she may not have even known who Peter was; rather than being filled with joy, she could have been filled with anger at the disruption. When we are working as unto the Lord everything we do becomes less like work. It really becomes an act of ministry. You are called by God to do a good work. Wherever He leads you, and in whatever He leads you in doing do it with joy, Colossians

3:23– Whatever you do, do it enthusiastically, as something done for the Lord and not for men.

Digging Deeper

1. Let's look again at some of the scriptures in this chapter: Philippians 2:14 --These verses tell us "Do all things without _____ or _____.

2. What is the purpose of working without grumbling or complaining (Phil. 2:15)?

   _____

   _____

3. Read Colossians 3:17- Write the verse our here. _____

   _____

4. Now, go back and read the all of Chapter 3 in Colossians and list as many of the works of Christ we are to possess when we become Christians. _____

   _____

   _____

   (I *will give you a little help here look particularly at verses 12-16*)

Pray This Prayer:

Lord begin a work in me so that my home is a reflection of Christ. Let others see that my work is as unto the Lord rather than man. Let my words be spoken without grumbling or complaining so that others will see the Glory of the Lord in and through me. Amen.

Design #10
"CRAFTER'S WELCOME"

Proverbs 31:19 - She stretches out her hands to the distaff, and her 1hands grasp the spindle.[27]

Over the years, I have done crafts of different types. There was a time in my life when my children were young that I loved to do cross-stitch. I would spend almost all of my spare time cross-stitching. I carried thread and cloth with me to work and when I had a break, I would cross-stitch. When I came home and the children were playing or in bed asleep, I would cross-stitch. I had a passion for cross-stitching. As time passed, my interest in cross-stitching was replaced by other craft projects. Now my hobby is scrapbooking. I love to take pictures and consider myself a very amateur photographer. I will take my photos, dress them up, and put them in keepsake albums. Someone once said to me, "who will care about all those pictures you have taken and put in all those albums?" (*I do most of them digitally now.*) It was a dreadful thought that no one would care to see my photographs, or that years from now my children and grandchildren won't even care to have them as memories of days long past. For me it has been a joy to preserve them this way. I would rather preserve them this way than just place them in a photo album. The digital ones are set to music, which is so nice. One day I will be gone, and those memories will be there for my children and grandchildren to enjoy. One of my most prized possessions is a quilt that my grandmother made. She is no longer with us, but I have

---

27

this quilt as a memory, and I can picture her sitting on her sofa with her quilt in her lap hand stitching each piece. It was something that she loved to do, and it showed in every quilt she made.

Again, we find that our "virtuous" woman is a woman who works with her hands. This verse tells us that she was busy making cloth. The New Living Translation says, "Her hands are busy spinning thread, her fingers twisting fiber." [28]

I want to give you a little history lesson about this job our "virtuous" woman is undertaking. I knew very little about the "distaff" or spinning, so I went searching (over the internet) to learn all I could about this early method of fabric making. In early history the distaff was the tool that was used to keep the fibers together prior to the spinning process. It could be a simple stick, a piece of rope tied to the waist, a belt, or a basket. Women would place a sufficient amount of flax, camel hair, goat's hair or the wool on or in the distaff for spinning. As they made their way to the market, they would carry the fiber in the distaff and would spin thread as they walked or, as they were setting visiting with each other. It was a common practice among women of all cultures. A woman's marital status was also identified by the color of ribbon she had attached to her distaff; often elaborate scenes were embroidered on the ribbon as an advertisement of her needlework skills. There were many varieties of distaff, signifying the region where the young woman was from. Some of them were hand carved by their fathers, or by prospective suitors, while others (such as the basket or belt) were used by women in different cultures.

The fiber that was to be spun was painstakingly cleaned and made ready to spin into thread. It had to be free of all debris before it was spun. The spinning process may not have been done at a spinning wheel. Thread making was done, most likely, as described in verse nineteen of Proverbs 31, by hand twisting the fiber in a continuous fashion. It wasn't until the 13th century that the wooden spinning wheel was invented. Now you have some idea about what it is that this woman had to go through just to obtain cloth for her family you may have a greater appreciation for her. I do! It reminds me of the hours that I spent cross-stitching. I would

---

28 Scripture quotations marked (NLT) are taken from the Holy Bible, New Living Translation, copyright 1996. Used by permission of Tyndale House Publishers, Inc., Wheaton, Illinois 60189. All rights reserved.

carry my pattern and my thread wherever I went and whenever I had the opportunity I was working on it.

Picture this scene in your mind with me. Here we find a woman who has sheared lambs for their wool or taken the fiber from the flax plant, (which was used to make linen), and now she must spin it into thread. Once the thread is made, she wraps it on the loom and weaves the cloth. Now that you have some idea about what this woman had to go through just to clothe her family, do you have a greater appreciation for her? I do! Can you imagine how much time it must have taken to make just one garment? This woman is amazing! How did she do that? God has given you unique gifts and abilities.

You may be thinking to yourself right now that you would love to have the time to do things that you love, but life is far too hectic to find any time for those things. Rick Warren, author of The Purpose Driven Life, writes; *God was thinking of you long before you even though about Him. His purpose for your life predates your conception. He planned it before you existed, without your input! You may choose your career, your spouse, your hobbies, and many other parts of your life, but you don't get to choose your purpose. The purpose of your life fits into a much larger, cosmic purpose that God has designed for eternity.*[29]

God has a plan for you. All you need to do is to find out what that plan is. I know what you are thinking because I have asked that question many times myself. Just what is my purpose in life and why am I here? I am still trying to figure that out. Very few of us will wake up and say, "I know just exactly what I am called to do" though some will. The ones that have had a call on their heart for a particular purpose in life attack each day knowing they are fulfilling that purpose. You and I may not know what we are going to do tomorrow, but we can know that our purpose is to glorify God. We can do that every day in *whatever* we do. The wise use of time is our biggest challenge. Too often, we don't have time because we don't make time. You can squeeze a few more moments out of your day with a little wise planning.

Here are a few suggestions that may help you in that area:

1. **Preparation.** Try jotting down in a notebook the things that you need

---

29   Rick Warren, The Purpose Driven Life (Grand Rapids; Zondervan, 2002), 21

to accomplish today. Write them all down. Once you have identified those things, check them off when you have completed them. I live by "post it" notes. I can't do anything if I don't write it down on a "post it". I stick them in my purse, in my car, and in my pocket, sometimes I keep a small notebook in my car to write notes to myself such as, call a friend, get a sympathy card, etc. You will find that simple steps like these can be helpful in giving you more time. You will be amazed at how much you get accomplished, but you have to stick to it. You will be so glad you did. One of the things that I have committed to doing is exercise. I have to make myself do it. There are many times I want to quit. In fact, many times I have quit and I know I need to exercise so I begin again. If I don't focus on what I know I need to do I won't take the time or make the effort to do it.

2. **Use what you have.** Your talents and your gifts are unique to you. There is not another person on the planet exactly like you. Even if you are a twin, there is something very unique about you. When I created my cross-stitch pictures, I had to follow a pattern, counting every square that I stitched. Each pattern required particular colors of threads, designed to make the finished product look just like the one in the picture. I was free to change those to colors of my choosing making those pictures uniquely mine. When I take a photograph, there is not another photograph taken by anyone else that is exactly like mine. Two photographers can stand next to each other, take a picture of the same scene, and yet have two distinctly different photographs. Why, because they each captured what they were focused on, and no two people focus on the same thing.

When I was reading about the distaff, I was very surprised at how many different types there were; each one was unique and they had different uses. Isn't that just the way God has made you and me-- unique and different? God has equipped us with different talents and different gifts but all with the same purpose, to glorify Him. Whether you are good at taking photographs, sewing, cooking, preparing taxes or balancing the checkbook, do it to the glory of the Lord.

3. **Don't waste time.** The women who made the threads for weaving had to make good use of their time. We have so many modern conveniences today that save us a lot more time. Don't waste your time sitting in front of the TV watching soap operas. Fill your mind with good things. If you are a stay-at-home mother, it can be so easy to put the kids down for a nap or send them to their rooms for an hour while you watch soap operas. I remember when my children were young and I stayed at home, almost all mothers watched soap operas. After each episode, we would call each other and talk about it. Not wanting to be left out, I soon found myself wrapped up in the soap opera saga forsaking my own family just to watch TV. Some women will record their favorite shows, while they are at work, and watch them when they get home. This is a real waste of your time. I am not saying that all television is a waste of time, but carefully choose what you will watch and limit the time you spend watching TV. Use your time wisely. Our "virtuous" woman doesn't waste her time, remember she is working while she is walking; she is buying and selling; she is sewing and baking; she is doing the taxes and paying the bills, and God has found favor with her. Her hands are not idol. She is a great homemaker. Her delight is in the things of the Lord and she loves serving her family.

I was in my office listening to a young mother who was complaining about not having any time for herself. Her spare time was never "spare" time. It was the time she did the laundry, cooked the meals, cleaned up after the children, and did the grocery shopping. By the end of the day she was too tired to give any time and attention to herself. I remember those days when all I did was take care of my family. God entrusted that job to me for that season of my life. I am a wife first, a mother second and my own person last. I wanted to tell her that one day she would have time for herself; but for now God has given her a tremendous job to do and that job is to care for her family. We are very self-oriented. We want to take long hot baths without the children knocking at the door screaming, "What's for supper?" We want to set down and read a book that has more than fifteen pages of colored pictures depicting cute little animals that talk like people. We want to have a conversation with another adult and talk about more than just what little Tommy or Susie did today.

I miss those days, when I could share the funny stories about the things my children did. I miss those days when the kids would run into the house after school and yell, "I made a *hundred* on my spelling test," and we would celebrate. I miss those cherished moments at the end of the day when my children would crawl into bed and fall asleep with the look of an angel on their face, and I would wonder how in the world something so rotten could be so precious. I miss baking cookies and making mud pies. I miss setting on hard bleachers cheering for my children as they played ball. I miss days when our whole family would go to the park, have a picnic and my children would swim until their skin wrinkled up like prunes.

Those days have provided many memories. Each memory has been etched into my mind. Some events have been captured on film for me to remember. God is allowing you to make memories that will forever be a part of who you are. All the dirty socks in the floor and the toys piled in the living room will fade into the sea of forgetfulness one day. All that will remain are those wonderful memories you created that brought you joy and happiness. Oh, there will be sorrow and pain, but the joy of being part of a family will far out way it, because that is what God does. He takes memories both good and bad, and turns them into something positive and beneficial. We just have to keep looking until we find them, waiting patiently for His timing.

Looking for a woman in the Bible who possessed this quality of a virtuous woman, I find myself studying Hannah, the mother of Samuel, once again. Not only was Hannah a woman of prayer, she was a mother. Her heart had longed for a child. She prayed earnestly for a child when God answered her prayers and gave her Samuel. Even though Hannah dedicated Samuel to the Lord she was still his mother. We read in scriptures that Hannah came to the temple year after year with a "little" coat for Samuel.

The fire was warm as Hannah sat in front of it. Her mind quickly wondered to her son, Samuel. He would soon have another birthday and she was thinking about what a fine boy he was, a true blessing from the Lord. How she missed watching him grow up. When she felt lonely, she knew that she could pay a visit to the temple to see him.

Samuel was a growing boy so he needed a new coat and Hannah was the one who would make it for him. She loved being his mother. Hannah began to think about the color of the coat that she would make him. Samuel liked bright color, but he was not a little boy anymore. She was sure that he would rather have a much more "manly" coat this year. "I will make it dark blue, the color of the night sky when the moon is full. I love that time of night, when it is quite; and you can see the moon and stars," she said aloud, as she wove the threads into cloth back and forth.

Elkanah, Hannah's husband; came in from tending to the flock of goats and sheep just in time to hear Hannah's discourse.

"Who are you talking too?" he asked, looking around the little house. He was familiar with every corner, and he knew there was no one there. He chuckled to himself. He loved Hannah and teasing her was part of their everyday life.

"Oh, hush! You know very well I was talking to myself," Hannah said as she set the loom aside and to retrieve the pot of stew she had prepared for their evening meal. "Get washed up. There is a basin of water and a towel ready for you to use. Then come and tell me how your day was and don't say a word about my conversation with myself," she said, giving Elkanah a playful tap on the arm.

After they finished their evening meal, Hannah moved back to her loom. "I want to get this fabric made and dyed by the morning so I can get started on the coat for Samuel. Since we will be leaving in two days to see him, I don't have a minute to lose. The days are getting cooler and it won't be long until he will need a new coat. That child is growing and I don't think he will be able to wear the coat I made for him last year. Besides I don't think his old red coat is "manly" enough for someone who's almost ten years old." Hannah said to Elkanah as she was weaved ferociously. Elkanah simply nodded his head knowing it was futile to try to get a word in when she was talking about her beloved Samuel.

This project was started much earlier when she began to spin the wool into thread. Every chance she had Hannah worked on it. She never thought about herself or how tired she was. Her love for Samuel and desire to meet his needs drove her to work many times into the wee hours of the morning. Nothing was too good for her son. Hannah wanted the coat to be made of good strong material so she carefully wove the fabric tightly. Finally, when she thought she had enough material to make a cost that would last Samuel through the whole year, she pulled if off the loom and began to mix up the dye. The anticipation *of seeing Samuel's face as she presented him with this gift drove her to work without much sleep over the next couple of days.*

Once she finished making the coat, Hannah wrapped it in a way that would keep it in perfect condition as they traveled. Nothing could have expressed her love for her son more than this. She could hardly contain the joy of knowing that this was the very day she would see her son.

What a devoted mother Hannah was. I think about my own son who is now a man. When he was away in the Middle East I wanted him to have things from home; things that would make him feel loved and a part of the family even though he was thousands of miles away. Those things may not mean much to him now, but I hope someday he will look back at some of those things and know how much he was and is loved. I can relate to Hannah. I, too, only see my son once or twice a year. When I see him, I want to do everything that makes him happy, like cooking his favorite foods or watching his favorite show on TV. Your family will always be your family. The little things you do will make a difference to them. God noticed Hannah's devotion and blessed her with two other children. He notices your devotion to your family as well.

DIGGING DEEPER

1. What lasting impression do I want to leave my family? _____

    _____

2. Look up the word preparation and write the definition here.

    _____

    _____

3. Read Proverbs 6:5-8. What can you learn from the ant? _____

    _____

4. Make a list of the things you are passionate about. _____

    _____

Pray this prayer:

Lord each day is Yours help me to make the best use of it for Your glory. Let my family see that I put their needs before my own. Help me to be devoted to You first then to my family. I give them back to you and pray that they will come to know and love you with all their heart. Amen.

Design # 11

"BRING ME YOUR TIRED AND POOR"

Proverbs 31: 20 -She extends her hand to the poor,
And she stretches out her hands to the needy.[30]

Remember the poem written by Emma Lazarus in 1908 "The New Colossus". The famous lines of that most of us learned in school.

"Give me your tired, your poor,
Your huddled masses yearning to breathe free,
The wretched refuse of your teeming shore.
Send these, the homeless, temptest-tost to me,
I lift my lamp beside the golden door."

In the New York Harbor stands the Statute of Liberty, a symbol of freedom to all who would see her. This statute was the creation of a sculptor named Frederic August Bartholdi. The statute was originally known as the "Liberty Enlightening the World" statute. In her left arm she holds a tablet that bears the date of the Declaration of Independence and at her feet is a broken shackle representing freedom. The seven spikes around her head represent the seven seas. Her right hand, held high in the sky, holds a torch that shines a powerful light at night, symbolizing a light shining on the world. Many Americans have only seen pictures of the Statute of Liberty in books or on television; many have never seen it in person, so for them it is merely a symbol, with little meaning. However, to those who

30

have crossed the seas to stand on America's shores it is a symbol of hope and freedom.

Our virtuous woman is a woman who knows hope and freedom, but they come from a different source. Her source of hope and freedom is the God of her salvation. She extends her hands to help the poor and less fortunate, not because of a statute, but because of a God who feeds the hungry, clothes the poor, gives sight to the blind, and healing to the sick. God's love moves her to act. Here we find this incredible woman ministering to the poor and needy. This is a picture of God's love working in her.

Today we have Christ's example, and His teaching about ministering to the poor and needy. Christ came to the poor and needy to bring salvation. In both Matthew and Luke, we read Jesus' own words as He talks about giving sight to the blind and preaching the gospel to the poor. What is the woman in Proverbs doing? She is bringing the love of God to those in need in tangible ways.

I am reminded of a something I heard Chuck Swindol say, "People don't care how much you know until they know hour much you care." This was not an original statement from him, but just as it had an impact on him, it had an impact on me as well. We can come to the poor with the gospel, but until we extend a helping hand, they are not as eager to listen.

Our virtuous woman was a missionary. She went out into the areas of town where the poor lived. She was a woman of means and her husband was a respected leader, yet she took the time to help those who needed it.

Let's get this down to a practical application for us. Do you have any opportunities in which you can minister to those who have less than you do? The answer to that question is most likely" yes", we all do. We all know of people less fortunate than we are. Ministering to the less fortunate requires giving something of ourselves. For most of us, we just don't want to get that close to poverty. We will give our money but not ourselves.

I want to share a beautiful story with you written by author and teacher Beth Moore. In her book "Further Still," she wrote about a time when she was waiting to board an airplane and was sitting alone reading when God spoke to her. There in the terminal humped over was a man in a wheelchair, dressed in clothes that didn't fit him. He had stringy, gray hair that hung down his back. He was a frightful looking man. While she sat there reading her Bible, God spoke to her, and told her that He wanted her to go and minister to him. Her first reaction was one that many of us would have, disbelieve. Surely, God would not be asking her to witness to *this* man, yet God continued to prompt her. He soon revealed that His intention was NOT for her to witness to the man, but rather to comb his hair for him. You can imagine her reluctance to do so. She pleaded with God to allow her to share the gospel anything but comb his hair. However, God's instructions were clear. "Beth, I want you to comb his hair." Not wanting to disobey God, she left the comfort of her world and moved towards the man. She stepped up the man in the wheelchair and asked him if she could brush his hair; and much to her surprise, he said, "If you want to." The man was heading home to see his wife. He had been in the hospital recovering from open-heart surgery and she had been too ill to visit him. He had not seen her in months. Beth asked him if he knew Jesus and his answer was *yes*. Both of them must have felt as if God had sent them to each other. There were hundreds of people in that airport that day, and because of Beth's willingness to be used by God, she was able to share the love of God with a flight attendant who witnessed the whole incident. Jesus commands to us are to feed the hungry, cloth the naked, and yes, comb someone's hair in His name.

That is what it means to "stretch out your hand to the needy." Would you or I have had the courage to answer God's call in that way? The Bible gives us a deeper look into God's heart for those who are in need.

- Psalm 9:18 - For the needy will not always be forgotten, Nor the hope of the afflicted perish forever.
- Psalm 12:5 - Because of the devastation of the afflicted, because of the groaning of the needy, Now I will arise," says the LORD; "I will set him in the safety for which he longs.
- Psalm 34:6 -This poor man cried, and the LORD heard him, And saved him out of all his troubles.
- James 2:5 - Listen, my beloved brethren: did not God choose the poor of this world *to be* rich in faith and heirs of the kingdom, which He promised to those who love Him?

What we have read and learned so far about the Proverbs 31 woman is that God wants us to have a willing heart, and a willingness to be yielded vessels. This wonderful woman cares for her home first then the needs of others. Here we see her opening her hands to help the poor and needy. She is a woman with a generous heart. She has received much from God and has much to give.

As a resident of Arkansas during Hurricane Katrina, I remember when many displaced victims of the storm came here. They were housed in church camps, and other facilities throughout the state. They were given necessities including food, shelter and clothing. Many people from our church gave up their Saturdays and/or evening to cook for them and to shuttle them into town where they could purchase things they needed. On one such occasion, my husband, Jim drove a van to town for them. I remember how some of our passengers were very appreciative of our help and others were not. Although we were there to help them, some of our guests seemed to be resentful, intimidating, and were very ungrateful of the assistance that had been given them. I had to remind myself that they did not come here by choice, and that they needed to see Jesus in our actions and in our faces.

There are times when, like Beth Moore, we want to argue with God about who we think actually deserves our help. We have no problem helping those less fortunate than us who are grateful and thankful. What about those who show no gratitude at all, those who do not care and feel as if they somehow deserve a hand out? Did Jesus minister to only those who were filled with love and gratitude? No, He came to seek and to save the lost, and that includes the unlovely.

The virtuous woman used what God had given her to help the poor and needy. She used her hands. God has already worked in her heart. He had prepared her for ministry. Many times we are reluctant to get our hands dirty. "Let someone else go", we argue. "Let someone else mingle with the poor." However, God looked down from heaven, saw our depravity and said, "I will send my son to mingle with the lost, which included you and me. I wish that I could tell you that in all my Christian life that I have walked the walk and talked the talk; that I fed the hungry, clothed the needy, and had a heart for God. Sadly, that has not been the case. There have been times in my own life when I sat in judgment of another person. God had to work in my heart before I could serve without judging them. Oh, I was willing to work, that was not the problem. The problem was that I was quick to judge the "poor" and the "needy" based on what I saw with my own eyes. I failed to see them with God's eyes. We need to be very honest here. God already knows what is in your heart and mine. Doing good for "goodness sake" is not what God wants. He uses our hands to *reach out* to others when we first *reach up* to Him for cleansing and direction.

So how do we get to be like this woman? Through prayer. You see, God knows what kind of person you are. He created you. He gave you the characteristics that are uniquely yours. He knows where your passions lie and what drives you to your knees in prayer.

When you pass by a homeless man, what is your first thought? Do you wonder what happened to make him homeless, or do you think, "He should just get out and find a job like the rest of us?" When you see a group of homosexuals picketing with signs for equality, do you pray for them, asking God to reveal their sin to them before it is too late? Or, do you feel disgust and hatred towards them for their choice to live this lifestyle? When you see someone dying of aids, do you judge them or feel compassion for them? When the church is feeding the hungry are you there dishing up food with a smile?

God knows what is in your heart. He knows that although you want to help the poor and needy, you haven't completely yielded yourself to His will. You are afraid. Afraid He might ask you to comb someone's hair or go to Africa as a missionary. Perhaps you're afraid that you're not "good enough" for God to use or that you won't be effective. The truth is that in and of ourselves, we are *not* good enough. We are human and we make mistakes. When we surrender our wills to God and let go of our fears, He can purify us and make us worthy vessels that are fit for His service.

Your journey begins at home. Who needs you the most is your family. They are the "needy." They need to witness your grace and loving kindness so they will know and be able to recognize the love of God. No matter where they go in life, once they are grown, it is what you have shown them as they were growing up that they will remember. It is a promise from God. Before you can show love and kindness to those *outside* your home, you must first display love and kindness *inside* your home. Your family is your first mission field. Next, begin to seek God for ways you can help the poor and needy in your community. Support unwed mothers programs by volunteering to counsel or give out clothing to their newborns. Give to mission projects in your own church. Donate food to food pantries. When God prompts your heart to move, don't ignore Him, there is a blessing waiting.

We are once again going to look at another Biblical example of a virtuous woman. Her name was Dorcas, which means gazelle, (a small swift animal that symbolized beauty and grace). Let's take a little trip back to Joppa and meet this incredible woman.

"Miriam, please take these cakes over to our sister Sarah's house. She has been so busy caring for her sick husband and I know she hasn't thought about getting any nourishment for her own body" said Dorcas as she dusted the flour off of her hands. "And, when you get back, dear, we will need to take these tunics over to JoAnna's house. She just doesn't have money to buy a new tunic, since her husband died last year."

Dorcus made her way to the kitchen to begin the dinner. "The Lord has been so good to me." she thought, "I love to sew even though these hands are getting old." Dorcus said out loud as she looked down at her hands. Her fingers were bent and calloused from years of working with them.

Miriam gathered the cakes and her shawl, covered her head and moved towards the door but before she could, two women from town came to the door. "Is Dorcas in?" one of them said to Miriam. Miriam simply nodded her head towards the kitchen, invited them in, and then made her way out into the street. Visitors were always stopping by unexpected, usually because someone was in need of help.

The two women made their way into the small kitchen where Dorcas was grinding wheat. "Good afternoon Dorcas," one of the women said as greeted Dorcas with a hug.

"Hello, my dear," Dorcas replied, "what brings the two of you here on this scorching summer afternoon?" Dorcus wiped her hands and offered her friends a cool glass of water.

"Do you remember Hannah, the daughter of Zebulum? She married Cornelius of Joppa and they live on the edge of town", began the elder of the two.

"Why yes of course," replied Dorcas.

"Well, her son became ill and he died. You know her husband died several

years ago, and he was her only child. She is in desperate need of a new cloak for the winter. It is already getting cool in the evenings and we thought you might be able to make one for her." "She has no close relatives and we wonder if you might be able to help."

"You are not going to believe this!" exclaimed Dorcus. "Just this morning I made three new cloaks, I had no idea whether or not anyone would need them. You know how much I love to sew; once I got started time flew by and before I knew it, I had made three of them."

They all laughed. Dorcus stood up and walked to the room where she slept and brought back one of the cloaks she had made that morning.

"Dorcus, we will never be able to repay your kindness," the two women said as they hugged her. Taking the cloak, they headed towards the street. "God bless you greatly, dear sister." (You can read this story in the book of Acts)

Dorcas lived in Joppa where she was known for her generosity and acts of kindness. Not much else is known about her. According to the book of Acts, the widows were recipients of her generosity. She made tunics and garments for them. When she became ill and died the news of her death reached Peter, who had heard of her generosity. He came to Joppa and when led to the upper room where her body was lying, the widows were standing by her crying, each one was telling the other how she had sewn something for them. Peter sent them out of the room and prayed over her body, telling her to rise up. He helped her to her feet and returned her to those who loved her, and whom she had cared for. The story does not go any further, but I believe she continued to minister to those widows in her care for many years to come.

What does this story say to you about the things that are important in your life? I have often thought of how my life will be remembered once I am gone. I don't want to be recognized for all the things I have done or accomplished during my life. I want my life to count for the Lord; I want it to make a difference in the lives of those I meet. In order for that to happen, I have to make some adjustments in the way I do things. My obedience to God in the way I "reach out" to my family could determine whether or not my children and/or grandchildren serve the Lord with all their hearts, souls and minds. Not to pat myself of the back and look at all the things I have accomplished because when I am gone what difference will it make? Their relationship to God is utmost important to me.

Our "reach" starts at home then extends out to the community. We can't control how others respond when we extend our hands. Our call is only to obey God and to follow His lead. Like everyone else on the planet. I'm not perfect nor do I have all the answers. But I have walked with God long enough to know that His smile and gentle embrace I feel when I've stepped out on faith and simply obeyed is worth a lot more than the little I may have given up to do so. Let go of whatever it is that you are holding in your hand so you can reach out and help others who need it.

Digging Deeper:

1. What can I do to minister to the poor and needy in my community? List a few of those here. _____
    _____
    _____

2. Read Luke 3:11. What are we commanded to do? _____
    _____ Do you have a heart for ministry to those less fortunate than you? _____

3. Can you think of someone in your church to which you could become a Dorcas? Write their name/s here. _____
    _____
    _____

Pray this prayer:

Father God, You love a generous spirit. You have blessed me with many wonderful gifts, my family, my home, my church. Help me to give of my time and resources to help those in need, so that Your Son may be glorified in my life and in theirs. Amen.

Design # 12

"LET IT SNOW, LET IT SNOW, LET IT SNOW."

Proverbs 31:21 - She is not afraid of the snow for her household, For all her household are clothed with scarlet.[31]

When I was a very young girl, my family moved to Newfoundland, Canada. This was a place where it snowed for months on end. It was not unusual for us to see five or six months of the white powdery stuff. I have some great memories of my time there.

There was one time in particular when we had a very unexpected snowstorm blow through, and I mean *blow through*.

Although my father was in the military, we lived in a small house outside the military base. I was in the first grade and my brother and I attended school on the base with the other "military brats" (as we were called.) While we were in class the storm came in fiercely, and the snow began to pile up quickly. So quickly in fact, that the school buses were not able to drive their usual routes to take all the students home. Those of us who lived off the base were stranded in the school without any way to get home to our families. After several hours of waiting, the school officials made arrangements with some of the families on the base to take us in until the roads had cleared. There were three other girls and myself who were unable to get home to our families, and we were fortunate enough to

31

stay with another classmate in her home. Her mother was gracious, and kind; she made our brief stay there more like a slumber party. We spent the night together in one room and made as cozy as a kittens, curled up by a fire. Even though the weather had altered our normal routine, we weren't afraid, anxious or nervous. Our needs were met, and we were well cared for until we were able to get home the next day.

While the weather in Canada could be harsh, as children we didn't seem to feel its threats. My mother made sure that we always had clean, warm clothes to wear, hot meals every night and a fire to warm ourselves by when we came in from playing in the snow. I do not remember worrying about such things because it seemed as though my mom was prepared for just about anything "Old Man Winter' could throw at her. She is a good example of the Proverbs 31 woman.

When I first considered the words in verse twenty-one, "she is not afraid of the snow." I was puzzled. Does it snow in the Middle East? I thought it was all desert: hot, windy and arid. However, I found that they actually do have a winter season, and in some places, it does snow. In fact, as I am writing this, the temperature in Jerusalem is fourteen degrees! Obviously, it does get cold and snow in Israel. As we dissect this verse, we notice this cold season does not cause her any alarm or fright. Why not? Because she has made provisions for her entire household; her husband, her children, and even her servants. We have already learned that she is quite the women when it comes to textiles. She spins thread, weaves cloth, and makes clothing. She most likely used wool to make her family warm clothes for the winter months as well. She is not in the least bit worried about her household going out into the cold weather. She has already prepared for it.

The Bible has a lot to say about preparation. You have already looked up the word prepare in the Webster's Dictionary and found that it means "to make ready before hand for some purpose, use or activity"[32] The word prepare or preparation is used 219 times in scripture. The importance of preparation was ingrained in the Jewish people. Each week they prepared for the Sabbath. There were many other feasts and holidays they had to prepare for; they often called them the "day of preparation." Why do

---

32 Merriam-Webster, I. 1996, c1993. *Merriam-Webster's collegiate dictionary.* (10th ed.). Merriam-Webster: Springfield, Mass., U.S.A.

you think God put so much emphasis on this? What do preparations tell others? When we prepare to entertain family and friends in our homes, why do we go to so much trouble? We usually plan an entire meal, purchase all the necessary ingredients, clean our house, and sweep the walkway to the front door. We do this because we want our guests to feel welcome. We want them to know that they are important to us, rather than an afterthought or nuisance. I believe this is what God is wanting from us. Our household should be our priority. Preparation says, "I love you, and you're important to me."

It is easy to see how the "virtuous" woman is a woman who is prepared. Notice the next part of this verse - "for her household is clothed in scarlet." I love the color red. My daughter has beautiful auburn hair, and I think it is the most beautiful color there is. Red is a symbol of royalty. Throughout history the color red was used to dress those who were rich and famous. In centuries past Kings and Queens usually had red in their robes.

Scarlet was the color of the dye obtained by the Egyptians from the shellfish Carthamus tinctorius; and by the Hebrews from the Coccus ilicis, an insect that infests oak trees, called kermes by the Arabians.[33] In the Old Testament, the high priest wore an ephod or linen apron made of gold, purple, and scarlet material. Rahab the harlot tied a **scarlet** ribbon in her window to signify the location of her family so they would be spared when the battle of Jericho took place. A **scarlet** robe was placed on Jesus as a mockery before his crucifixion. Scarlet was used extensively for the tabernacle furnishings. (Exodus 26:1 –"Moreover you shall make the tabernacle with ten curtains of fine twisted linen, and blue and purple and scarlet *material;* you shall make them with cherubim, the work of a skillful workman.")

Our "virtuous" woman dressed her family in the finest garments she could afford. I don't believe she did this as a way to flaunt her wealth, but rather as a way to reveal their value to her. What we see here is a woman who spares nothing to see to it that the needs of her family are met, not only her immediate family, remember she clothed the entire household in these clothes. I would imagine that the majority of us do not have servants living with us in our homes. We do however; have people who serve us

---

33   Easton, M. 1996, c1897. *Easton's Bible dictionary.* Logos Research Systems, Inc.: Oak Harbor, WA

regularly. We all have the postal carrier, the grocery clerk, etc. Do we value them as we should? I challenge you to take the time to notice your "servants." Do they have decent shoes? Are their clothes in need of repair? If you have the means, "clothe them in scarlet." Let them know they are important to you.

As I think about giving my best to those God has entrusted into my care, as well as those whose lives I come in contact, with I am reminded of the words of Jesus when told his disciples; "In My Father's house are many dwelling places; if it were not so, I would have told you; for I go to *prepare* a place for you. "If I go and *prepare* a place for you, I will come again and receive you to Myself, that where I am, *there* you may be also." (John 14:2-3) God has His very best waiting for us and we are His invited guests. Don't you love knowing that God has reserved a seat for you at His table?

Let's look at a woman, from the book of Mark, who gave what she had to give. You may already be familiar with her. She was a widow and she came into the temple with two small coins that amounted to about one penny.

The streets were crowded with families all making their way to the temple that day. Among them was a widow who had been pushed several times because she was old and slow. This didn't seem to bother her; she had many thoughts running through her mind. She remembered the times that she and her husband had come to the temple together. A smile crossed her face as she thought of him. Although he was gone, she wasn't angry with God for taking him. She had a deep and personal relationship with God and was truly grateful for the years they had together, and for the children and grandchildren who were still with her. "I must get to the temple before dark." She thought. She paused and wrapped her tattered shawl around her shoulders. In her hand she held two small coins, worth very little money, but all she had. "God has blessed me in so many ways," she thought. She remembered when she needed oil for her lamps how God provided, and when she needed flour for her evening meal there always seemed to be enough.

Once she reached the temple, she could see the multitudes of people going up the steps to the treasury and she watched as they made huge contributions, making a big production out of their giving. Soon it was her turn and she moved towards one of the trumpet-shaped, chests placed around the court-of-

women, and without any fan fair placed her two small coins in the chest. No one even noticed her, so she thought.

"Do you see that woman over there?" Jesus asked the disciples as He pointed towards the widow who had just deposited her offering. The disciples did not see her and shook their heads no at Jesus' question. "I tell you the truth, this poor woman has given more than all the others put together here today. For they only give out of their wealth, but she has given out of her heart all that she had and has put everything she has into the chest."

The widow offered a prayer for her children and grandchildren and turned to go back to her home, not realizing that Jesus had taken notice of her faith and her giving.

Can you picture in your mind what it must have been like for her on that day? I like to think that she was a gentle, sweet, "grandmotherly-type" woman. I can picture her getting up that morning and going about her day having a small "cake" of bread for her meal before she headed to the temple to honor God. She had no idea that Jesus and His disciples were going to be there. Jesus used her simple act to teach His disciples (and us) what it means to truly give.

Perhaps you don't fear, the "snow" and harsh weather. Maybe you don't have "scarlet" to clothe your family. We are all at different stations in life and have various resources available to us. I believe God's message to us is that He is not as concerned with the amount we give but with the attitude behind our giving. Quit comparing your "household" to the Jones' and just give them your best. Don't be like the people in the temple and brag about how much you spend on things for your family. That does not honor God. Show your family and others that you love them by preparing for each season. Take what you **do** have and make them feel like royalty.

DIGGING DEEPER:

1. In what ways are you preparing for you families physical needs?

_____

2. Read John 14:2 - In my father's house are many mansions, if it were not so _____ have told you so, for I go to _____ _____ a _____ for you.

3. The word *prepare* in Hebrew is *kuwn* which means to be firm, to be established, securely determined, ready. Now Read Psalm 65:9 God prepared the earth to _____ people with _____.

4. Read the following verses and draw a line to verse the best describes the use of scarlet within the verse.

   String used to signify first-born   Isa. 1:18
   Shields of warriors   Gen. 38:28
   Color in the ephod (worn by priests)   Ex. 28:6
   Sins as Scarlet   Nahum 2:3

PRAY THIS PRAYER:

Lord, I love my family and I am thankful that you have placed them in my life. Give me wisdom in making the proper preparations to meet their needs in a way that brings honor and glory to You. Let them see that I love you first so that I may love them best. Let them see the work of Your hands in all that I do. Amen.

Design #13

"The Sewing Circle"

Proverbs 31:22 She quilts her own bedspreads. She
dresses like royalty in gowns of finest cloth.[34]

When I think of this verse, my mind immediately goes to my grandmother. She loved to make quilts. All of her children and grandchildren wanted to have one of her quilts, and when she passed away so did her gift of quilting. No one else in the family ever learned the art of quilting. I can remember times when she would be sitting in her living room piecing a quilt together by hand. It is a rare art form among woman today.

How does this verse 22 apply to us in the 21st century? Our lives are very different compared to those who lived 2000 years ago. Our modern conveniences make sewing outdated for the most part. We don't have to make our own clothing anymore; we can go to the department store and buy them. So, how in the world does this apply this to our lives today?

I have to laugh here, because I was just thinking about a time in my own life when I made my very first dress. I was in the seventh grade and like most girls; I took Home Ec. The first half of the year we spent learning to cook, and the second half of the year we had to learn to sew, or at least make an attempt at it. My mother helped me pick out material and a pattern to make a dress. It was a simple pattern, or so I thought, but it had to have a zipper. I was mortified! A zipper? I thought, "I can't sew in

34

a zipper," and I was right. When it came time for me to add the zipper to the dress, I did not sew it in correctly. I had to take it out and start over. It was taking f-o-r-e-v-e-r to remove every stitch from that zipper. I had a wonderful, bright idea. The tool I was using to remove the zipper was called a "seam ripper", and as you can imagine, I decided I would just try to rip out the zipper with one fell swoop. When I did, I ripped a six-inch tear in the material. There was no way to fix that so I had to start all over with a new pattern and of course another zipper! After blood, sweat and some tears I finished the dress, I think I might have even worn it a time or two. Over the years, I have only attempted to make my own clothes a few times and for good reason. I never liked what I made. However, my best friend did and she loved the fact that she got all of my clothes at a real bargain. She was always asking me when I was going to have another yard sale.

Our Proverbs 31 woman was not at all like me. She was a great seamstress. Her clothing was made of the finest silks and dyed the colors of royalty. She was a strikingly beautiful woman, well dressed and very much a lady.

After my experiences, I have a completely new respect for women who can sew. When I was a young girl, my mother made most of my clothes. Whenever I needed something new to wear, we couldn't just go out and buy it because our income wouldn't allow it; instead, my mother would make it. Although she was a very good seamstress herself, and was able to duplicate anything I saw in the stores, I knew my clothes were not "store bought." I have to admit that I was not very fond of "handmade" clothing. I wanted to have a "store bought" outfit, just like all the other girls in school. In my childish ignorance, I did not appreciate what my mother had done for me.

Not only does our "virtuous" woman know how to sew for her family, she makes quilts too! She is quite a woman. How could we ever possibly live up to her? She can cook, sew, and manage the family business, and buy and sell property. Not to mention that the people in her household are among the best dressed in town, and she looks like royalty. How does she do it? How does this woman pull it all off? That is the question on everyone minds. We are going to explore this verse and see.

"She makes coverings for herself." The word *covering* here in this text is the word *marbad*, which means a *covering of tapestry or a spread*. Two things come to my mind when I see this definition. The <u>spread</u> would be similar to our quilts or a bedspread, and <u>tapestry</u> would be that of a fine woven wall hanging. I did a little research and found that tapestry wall hangings were created in hundreds of designs often in various sizes. These tapestries hung on the walls as decoration. A tapestry was actually a woven decorative fabric with the design built up in the weaving process. What does that remind you of? It reminds me of my grandmother's quilts. She would set out with a pattern in mind, although she wasn't weaving the fabric, she was creating a design throughout the course of each piece. The final product was exquisite in detail and design.

A few years ago, Jim and I traveled to North Carolina to see the Biltmore Mansion. Hanging on the walls in the formal dining room were fifteen to twenty large tapestries. These tapestries needed to be taken down from time to time and repaired by hand, because time had taken a toll on the threads, and the tapestries were showing significant wear. Each one was carefully cleaned and maintained, then hung back on the walls for all the visitors to enjoy. During our tour of the home, no flash photographs were allowed to be taken because of the damage the light from a flash would do to the fabrics. Each tapestry was magnificent creation with fine detail.

The "covering", I believe our "virtuous" woman is referring to, in verse 22 is the covering for her bed- her bedspread. Why do you think that making a bedspread has gotten attention of the author? Here is a thought?

The bedroom is our haven of rest, the place in our home where we spend a lot of time. It is the place where you can curl up with a great book, spend time with your "honey", and read bedtime stories to your children. I am reminded, again, of my grandmother and her quilts. One year for Christmas my mother and father bought one of my grandmother's quilts and gave it to me. After she gave me the quilt, I was afraid to put it on my bed. I did not want anything to happen to it, so I tucked it neatly away in a closet. When my grandmother died, I wanted to display the quilt she had lovingly made for me so, I placed the quilt on the bed in my guestroom. As time has gone by, I have taken the treasured quilt, wrapped it up, and placed it once again in the closet. It is something I want to preserve to pass down to my grandchildren someday. Are you beginning to get a picture of this woman in your mind? I know I have. She is a thoughtful, kind, loving, thrifty, smart, generous and compassionate woman. Who cares for the needs of her household as well as those less fortunate.

Do you see where her priorities are? She has taken care of everyone else before she has taken care of herself. However, she does take care of herself. Many women neglect themselves. Some women feel as though they lost their identity when they had children. They will pour their whole lives into their husbands and children and neglect themselves. I want to encourage you here. Do not do that! If you do not take care of your physical, spiritual and emotional body, who will? God created you and you are priceless to Him. How would you care for something that had that kind of value? If you are one of those women, you need to stop neglecting yourself. You are a daughter of the King of Kings and Lord of Lords! Now go out and get a manicure and put on some lipstick, it's okay!

The "virtuous" woman was a woman of means; she had servants, her husband was known at the city gates. She was a shrewd businesswoman, and she dressed the part. Now I want to stop and park here for just a moment. Please don't get the impression that because she had money, and position she flaunted that in the community. That is not what God is showing us as we study this woman. When we walk into a room, I believe that God wants us to carry ourselves with dignity and grace, to be thought of as "ladies". Far too often we do not carry ourselves with dignity and we do not act like a lady. Remember WHO you are and WHOSE you are!

I love the movie *"My Fair Lady"* starring Aubrey Hepburn. You may remember the story. A dignified scholarly Englishman makes a wager with a colleague that he can make a "lady" out of any rough, undignified female. Audrey Hepburn played the role of the rough-around-the-edges young girl, from the other side of the tracks, who is transformed into a beautiful, refined, elegant lady under the tutelage of this English scholar. I believe this is what God has in mind for his most prized creation. When Adam laid eyes on Eve for the first time, I doubt very much that she was wearing sweat pants, a holey T-shirt and fuzzy slippers. I doubt that she had her hair pulled up in a twisted mess and clipped to the top of her head either. If she had, I think Adam would have asked God for a "do-over."

God made us. He wants us to reflect His character not only in what we do and say, but also in how we look. Let me say this. When you get up in the morning, if you don't have to go to work, don't sit around the house in you pajamas until mid-morning. Don't greet your family at the end of the day looking like you have been stranded on an island for days without any soap and water. Get dressed, put on your makeup and fix your hair. Some of you women are blessed with beautiful skin and don't need makeup, but for the rest of us we need all the help we can get, and if that means putting on a little makeup, then we need to do just that. I have made it a practice never to leave my house without my hair fixed and my makeup on, or being properly dressed. I realize that there will be times when you are working in the yard and you need to run to the nursery for more topsoil or flowers and you don't want to take the time to get "fixed up." I am not talking about those times; I am talking about your appearance in general.

My husband knows that when we go into town on Saturday morning he needs to give me plenty of time to get ready. He knows that I am not going out in public looking like I just got out of bed and threw something on, and that I don't care who I may see. The "virtuous" woman cares about her appearance. She makes it a point to dress appropriately, which brings me to the next point we need to address– that of the proper attire. It seems with every new year of fashion we see less and less modesty in young women's clothing, which leads to seeing more and more of young ladies bodies.

We read in the scriptures in *1 Timothy 2: 9-10 Likewise, I want women to adorn themselves with proper clothing, modestly and discreetly, not with braided hair and gold or pearls or costly garments, but rather by means of good works, as is proper for women making a claim to godliness.* The contrast here is one of worldliness versus godliness. In the Bible Exposition Commentary by author Warren Weirsbe, he writes:

A woman's clothing should be decent, orderly, and in good taste. "Shamefacedness" literally means "modesty, the avoidance of extremes." A woman who possesses this quality is ashamed to go beyond the bounds of what is decent and proper. "Sobriety" comes from a Greek word that means "having a sound mind and good sense." It describes an inner self-control—a spiritual "radar" that tells a person what is good and proper. Paul admonished the Christian women to major on the "inner person," the true beauty that only Christ can give. He did not forbid the use of nice clothing or ornaments. He urged balance and propriety, with the emphasis on modesty and holy character. [35]

---

35 Wiersbe, W. W. 1996, c1989. *The Bible exposition commentary.* Victor Books: Wheaton, Ill.

I must confess I enjoying shopping for a new outfit. I want to dress nice and I want to keep in fashion as much as modesty, good taste, and my budget will allow. It is hard sometimes to find things that I feel are appropriate to wear. I do not want to look "frumpy" but I do not want to look "provocative and suggestive" either. There is a balance and our "virtuous" woman has found it. We are Christ's representatives in this world. How we dress tells the world what we think of who we are in Christ. Either we can spend too little time and money on our appearance, or we can go to the opposite extreme and spend too much time and money on our appearance. The *key* is balance. As I sit here writing, I am convicted about what the Bible has to say about adorning ourselves on the outside en lieu of focusing on the inside. I am afraid we might miss something very important as we study this extraordinary woman. Remember that we learned she was frugal. She could have bought anything she wanted yet she chose to make her clothing herself. Not only did she sew for herself, but as we have seen in previous verses, she took care of her servants as well. Being conscious of her family's needs, she made sure they were taken care of before her own. Why? Because of love.

Elizabeth George in her book "Beautiful in God's Eyes" writes:

The Proverbs 31 woman who is beautiful in God's eyes is a weaver, but you are a weaver, too. You can weave your own tapestry of beauty right in your own home—wherever home is. What will you need? In a word, love. With threads of love woven by hands of love and expressing a heart of love, you can creatively transform even a camper into a home.[36]

We can spend a lot of time trying to look good and have a beautiful home, but if we fail to express love for our families in tangible ways, we will miss something very important that God wants to teach us. Proverbs 31:30 tells us that "charm is deceitful and beauty if vain." Without balance, we will not properly handle the external things in our lives.

Once again, we are going to look at another personification of the Proverbs 31 woman and her name in Lydia. She is a businesswoman who deals with fine quality fabrics: linen, silk and those dyed with expensive dyes, usually deep scarlets and purples. However, that is not what makes her a virtuous woman. In order to see her virtuous qualities we have to go

---

36 George, Elizabeth, 1944- Beautiful in God's Eyes, Harvest House Publishers. Eugene, OR

back to where we first meet her, and put ourselves in her shoes. What was life like for Lydia and why did God see fit to mention her in scripture?

Lydia was known for her skilled business sense. Her success was known throughout Philippi. She was the head of her household, possibly a widow or she may have always been single. What we do know about her it that she was a "seller of purple" Let's look at what Lydia was doing when she encountered Paul and just what made her a virtuous woman. Her story can also be read in the book of Acts.

It was a hot, dusty day, and Lydia was laying out the beautiful linen, flax and wool fabrics in the booth at the marketplace. As always, she took great care in placing the finest cloth out for everyone to see. She had several wealthy customers who were sure to be in the marketplace today. She had taken great pride in her fabrics that were hand dyed with the finest dyes available. Dyes from the rind of pomegranates made the most beautiful blue shades. The best red and scarlet dyes came from the grubs that fed on the oak trees and were very hard to come by. She knew how to work "magic" with these dyes, and her fabrics were used to make clothes for the most prominent people in town. She was proud of her work.

It was a slow day for trading and Lydia found herself listening to the merchants and the patrons in the marketplace. She overheard one of them say there would be a man named Paul from Tarsus speaking down by the river. Lydia was a God-fearing Gentile who knew the words of Moses and Abraham. She wanted to hear what Paul had to say as he opened the Shema and spoke the words of Abraham.

She decided to close up early in order to make it to the river before it became too crowded. The news about Paul had spread throughout the city. She wanted to hear Paul speak and hoped that he would read from the Talmud. "What sort of man is he?" she thought as she folded up the fabrics and placed them in the baskets she used to transport her fabrics to and from the small house she lived in.

It was a beautiful, cool afternoon, so Lydia decided she would take along one of her blankets and some fruit. If it were not too crowded, she would sit by the river's edge and take in the sunshine and blue skies.

Lydia was not prepared for what she would hear. She had expected Paul to read about Abraham, Isaac, and Moses, or tell about how God had led the children of Israel out of Egypt. She had heard those stories time and time again but she never got tired of them. Today was no different, and her heart was stirred as she listened to Paul preach about a man named Jesus. She had heard of him but never before had she felt so drawn to the Master, Jesus. Lydia had strong beliefs, but when Paul spoke, it seemed as though she was hearing it for the first time. God was working in her heart. After the meeting, Lydia pushed her way through the crowd to speak to Paul. Her reputation allowed her to move through the crowd with little trouble. Once she got close enough, she spoke to Paul "May I ask you a few questions about the man you were speaking of today?" Paul sensing the work of God moving in her heart led her away from the crowd.

"What would you like to ask me?" Paul spoke his voice filled with compassion.

"I have heard stories about a man named Jesus. Are they true?"

"Yes, I used to deny that Jesus was the Messiah, I persecuted Christ-followers, and then one day on the road to Damascus my life was changed." Paul shared his own conversion story with Lydia. He continued, "Jesus is God's Son, He came to seek and save that which was lost. Every one of us are like sheep that have gone astray. Our lives are full of sin that separates us from God. Jesus bore all our sins on the cross so that we could become children of God." Paul watched as tears filled Lydia's eyes. He knew that God was stirring in her heart so he asked her a simple question, "Lydia, do you believe Jesus is the Messiah and that he came to save not only the Jews but the Gentiles?"

"For many years I would listen as the Jewish Rabbi's spoke of the coming of a Messiah, I believe He has come and that his name is Jesus. You have opened my eyes that I may see and my ears that I may hear, now what must I do to be saved."

Paul took Lydia's hands in his and they prayed together. Lydia was so compelled by the love of Christ that she was converted right there.

"Would you come to my house tonight and tell my family what you have told me so that they might believe? Lydia asked.

Paul was moved by her new found love for Christ so he agreed. Lydia could not contain her excitement. She turned away from Paul and began to run quickly through the crowd of people who were still gathered by the river's edge. Many of them turned to see Lydia running, almost skipping, through the crowd. "What in the world had come over her?" they thought.

As evening came, Paul arrived at Lydia's home just as he had promised.

After the evening meal, he began to tell them the story of Jesus. Hearing Paul's words, and seeing the joy on Lydia's face, they too were converted. Lydia became a great witness to the goodness and mercy of Christ. Daily as she worked in the marketplace selling her fabric she remained steadfast in worship and followed Paul's missionary journey with great interest. She opened her home to him on many occasions. Paul knew that whenever he was in Philippi, he would spend time with Lydia and her household.

Lydia was a woman of influence, yet she risked it all to follow Christ. She lived in a town that was largely hostile to the work of Christ and to the followers of Christ. She remained a faithful follower. Just as Lydia wove fabrics, and dyed them with rich, vibrant color Christ also weaves a tapestry of vibrant colors within our hearts. The colors of, His grace, mercy, love and kindness. Lydia understood that, and so can we. He longs to create a beautiful work of art in the heart and lives of his children. As women, we can understand this type of analogy. We love the beauty of a sunset. We love to walk through fields of flowers. We will sit for hours, hold a tiny baby, and marvel at their perfection. God made us that way. He wove himself in and through our lives.

Digging Deeper

1. Read Ephesians 2:10 You are a _____ of Christ. How are you weaving those same principles into my family's lives? List them here. _____

    _____

    _____

2. Is it evident to all who know me that I love God first? Yes _____
    No_____

3. Read Revelations 2:4 and Matthew 22: 37, What is the first-love referred to in this passage? _____

    _____

4. Galatians 5:22 describes the fruit of the spirit. These are reflections of Christ in you. List below the nine fruits of the spirit listed in this verse. Which of those words best describes the reflections of God's love displayed in you? (You *may have several, list them all, but be honest*)

_____

_____

PRAY THIS PRAYER:

God, as a woman designed and created by You, let my actions be filled with grace, and loving kindness to all those I come into contact with. Let my life become a rich tapestry of your grace to a lost world. Weave in and through my life the threads of gentleness, a quiet spirit, self-control, love and patience. Let me see the beauty in simple things. Teach me to walk in your ways, step by step as You lead me.

Design #14

"To Love, Honor and Respect"

Proverbs 31:23 Her husband is greatly respected when he deliberates with the city fathers.[37]

What is your husband known for among the people in your church, your community, or within the circle of your closest family members and friends? The "virtuous" woman's husband had a reputation for being well known. When his name was mentioned in conversation at the city gates, everyone knew who he was. Not only was he well known, but he was also respected. That is a very important word in this verse. The word *respect* means highly regarded. What does that mean to a man? Everything. One of the greatest needs is respect. They want to be respected in the workplace, in the home, in the church and in the community. Women we play a very important role in either making or breaking their reputation. As I mentioned in a previous chapter I feel that women do a great deal to boost their husbands or to tear them down. I must admit when I was younger, I did not take care of my husband's reputation. I did not guard my words to elevate him and lift him up in the "gates." Think, if you will, about a moment in your own life when you may have been guilty of this yourself. Does this sound familiar to you?

"Susan, I am so upset with my husband! You will never guess what he did last night. He made me so angry that I was ready to pack my bags and take the children to my mothers."

37

"Why, Ann, what in the world did he do?

The next thing you know, you have gone into a long dissertation about all the things that your husband is "guilty" of doing. You have torn him to shreds right there at the water cooler in front of your peers. His reputation has been shattered, and those people will have a hard time seeing him with respect ever again. Whatever your husband did that may have hurt you, and made you want to run to your mother, should only be shared with someone you trust for sound advice. Sharing that with everyone in the office is not the appropriate place.

We all have moments in our lives where the other person has done, or said something that hurt our feelings. Most of the time, (not always, but most of the time) when the two of you sit down and discuss what took place, those things can be resolved. Notice I said the "two of you" not the five of you: your husband, you, Martha, Sue and Linda (from the office).

I can tell you from personal experience that "group discussions" about "personal matters" does nothing to elevate your husband's reputation with them. In fact, it does just the opposite.

Several years ago when I was going through my most difficult days, (the days before my divorce), I was guilty of tearing down the reputation of my ex-husband. I felt justified in doing so; after all, I was the victim, or so I told everyone. I felt as if I needed to let the world know what was going on in my life, so I could gain their sympathy and make me look like the "martyr" for suffering through my marriage at the time. Let me interject something here. In no way am I suggesting that if your husband is doing something that is morally wrong or physically abusive, you or your children that you should not get counsel. In fact, I **encourage** you to do so. What I *am* suggesting is this: if you find yourself in those circumstances, you should definitely speak up. Those times are critical for you to get counsel, *wise* counsel. Not counsel from your friends in the break room or over a hamburger at the local fast food restaurant. Your friends may not be able to be objective and lend the right kind of support for you. You need to talk with a professional counselor or pastor.

Now, for those times when your husband is simply being human, and you feel like doing a little "husband-bashing," stop. Stop and think about what you are doing to his reputation and to the respect given by those he works and comes in contact with on a regular basis. I make it a practice now not to say negative things about my husband to anyone. I mean *anyone.* Is he perfect? No. Do others think he is perfect? No, but it is not because I have painted him in a negative way. My job is to lift him up and encourage him to be the very best person that God wants him to be. I am to be his biggest fan, **intentionally!** I want others to value him for the person God has created him to be. If I am constantly badgering him in front of others, then I have done absolutely the opposite of respecting him. I have dishonored him, and more importantly, I have dishonored God. It is not my place to tear him down in front of others or behind his back. There will be times when he comes in from work after having had the worst day ever. If you "let him have it" for leaving his dirty socks in the middle of the floor, for not picking up the newspaper, or for letting the grass grow too long, you have dishonored him as the head of your home and as a man. Ladies guard your words about the man that you made a life-long commitment to. If you will do this, you will boost his self-esteem more than you will ever know.

How is your husband seen in the community? Verse 23 describes him as a pillar in the community; and not only do people respect him, but they respect his wife as well. Why do you think that would be important? Think about people that you know, men and women that you admire. What is it about them that you admire? Do you admire them for their money, their position, their home, or the kind of car they drive? Do you admire them for their character, their integrity, their love for each other and for God? Is that why you admire them? If so, you will understand why God chose to mention this aspect of His design in this verse of Proverbs 31. After all, we are talking about her, not him, so why did he mention the husband in this verse?

Warren Weirsbe in his *Expository Outline of the New Testament* writes: [38] "*Man and woman both have a place in the economy of God, and when either one steps out of place, there is confusion and trouble. Of course, the headship of the man does not mean dictatorship; rather it means example and leadership in love.*" The husband and the wife complement each other.

As I mentioned earlier, I enjoy shopping — I always have. But just as important the outfit is, I think my accessories are also important. Stay

---

38 Wiersbe, Warren W.: *Wiersbe's Expository Outlines on the New Testament.*
    Wheaton, Ill. : Victor Books, 1997, c1992

with me here! My husband was with me on a shopping trip and picked out a dress for me to try on. He liked it so we bought the dress and took it home. After we got home with it, I started thinking about what shoes I would wear, what necklace and earrings would look good with it, all of the accessories that would complement the dress. My husband realized that it was not just about the dress. When I wore the dress with the shoes and other accessories no one noticed or even commented on the dress, only "how cute my shoes were." Now it is sort of a joke around our house that if I buy something new to wear I make sure that I have the right accessories to go with it. The shoes I wore complimented the dress. Complimented not took away from the dress. Even my husband noticed. As wives we are to be just like that with our husbands. We are to compliment him. Not only are we to say complimentary things to others about him, we are to be a compliment to him in the way we represent ourselves.

Proverbs 31 tells us her husband was known at the gates, but he also sat with the elders. He was a prominent man in the city. A leader in the community and you can bet that his wife was also well known. Whether or not your husband has a position of leadership in the church or the community, you must guard his reputation and your own. It is said that behind every good man is a great woman. That is true. You are to be his cheerleader, his confidant, and his best friend. When you are his helpmate you free him to excel at work or in other positions where is he called upon to be a leader. When he is freed from financial worry or knowing that you are taking care of things at home this is of great value to him. You are then being a compliment to him. When there is order in the home, people know that there is harmony between the husband and the wife. They truly are "one" person: thinking as one, working as one, and loving as one.

Think how freeing that would be for you and for your husband. As he serves, so should you. Look for ways that the two of you can serve in your church together. There are many ministry opportunities that both of you can do together: work together in the children's areas, as greeters, singing in the choir or teaching a Sunday morning class together. These couples are co-laborers in Christ and it is beautiful to watch them work together. Others will notice too. They will see that you are *real* partners in the truest since of the word. I love to see husbands and wives working in the church together

Ruth Bell Graham, wife of Billy Graham was one such Proverbs 31 woman. She was "the woman behind the man." Billy Graham said this about his wife

"I have been asked the question, "Who do you go to for counsel, for spiritual guidance?" My answer: my wife, Ruth. She is a great student of the Bible. Her life is ruled by the Bible more than any person I've ever known. That's her rule book, her compass. Her disposition is the same all the time—very sweet and very gracious and charming. When it comes to spiritual things, my wife has had the greatest influence on my ministry."—**Billy Graham**

Ruth Graham was born in China, the daughter of Missionaries. When she came to the United States she attended college in Wheaton, Illinois where she met and later married Billy Graham in 1943. For a brief time she served as a pastor's wife before her husband moved to serve as an evangelist in the Youth for Christ ministry and later, full-time in the Billy Graham Evangelistic Association. She was a writer and biblical scholar, the author of many poems and book. Although they served side by side, Billy was the one who people recognized. She never complained about the complexities of being the wife of a traveling evangelist. Instead, she was content to be a wife and mother. Ruth was Billy Graham's strength and partner all the years of their marriage. She was proud of her husband and his reputation was safe in her care. They were an incredible team who served the Lord together. Billy Graham once said that he and his wife were called. God calls both husband and wife to be a team that serves together— whether or not you are in the same location geographically.

We are not all going to be called to be wives of evangelists or even pastors, but, we are called to minister *with* our spouse and *beside* him. Ruth Graham longed to serve the Lord as a missionary and was continually reminding herself that God *had* given her a mission field at home; and that is exactly where she faithfully served Him all of her days. Isn't that what we all want to have said of us, we faithfully served God all of our days, and we were obedient to God's call to work along side our husband? If God calls you to serve in a ministry that he is not directly involved with, such as Women's Ministry, you must have the support of your husband. My husband is my biggest fan, when I am working with a Women's Ministry project I know that I can count on his help, if I need it. I know that he is cheering me on, also. It goes back to complimenting each other.

The scriptures are rich with examples of godly women. They provide us with examples of ordinary women who struggled to fulfill the calling of God upon their lives. One such woman was Sarah, the wife of Abraham. What can Sarah teach any of us about the Proverbs 31 woman?

Sarah, the very name means *Princess*, but how could Sarah ever be considered a princess. She was sixty-five years old when her real journey began. A journey that would call her to leave her homeland, the people she loved, and follow this man, Abram, wherever he would go. God had promised Abram that he would be a "great nation." How was that to be accomplished, given the fact that she herself had bore him no children? Even the people within their camp who knew of the promise from God were laughing at such a notion. Let's take a look at her life for a moment.

"Sarai, it is time for us to leave." Abram said as he gently pulled her along. "We have a long journey ahead of us, but God will go before us."

Sarai remembered the words "God will go before us" as she thought back on the day that they said good-bye to family and friends. It had been a long time ago. She missed the comfort that she felt when she was laughing and talking with her friends. She loved Abram, and would gladly follow him wherever he went. She had been a good wife to him all these years. But, there was something missing in her life.

She watched as the servant's children were playing near the tent and how their mothers were close by, making sure they were never out of their sight. The emptiness of never holding her own child was magnified with every hug given to one of those children by their own mother. Oh, the children loved Sarai. She made them cakes and told them stories. She laughed and played with them, but none of them called her mother. Sarai knew that it was impossible for her to know the thrill of motherhood. That time in her life had passed, so she must be content with this reality.

It was nightfall, and once again, Sarai was feeling the pain of her barrenness. Abram sensed that there was something wrong and moved close to her and questioned, "Something is troubling you tonight; what seems to be the matter?"

"Am I a good wife to you, Abram?" Sarai asked gazing off.

"Of course, why do you ask?"

"Why then has God seen fit to leave me childless?

"Sarai, why are you not content to just simply be my wife? Why do you always seek that which you cannot have? Do I not make you happy?" Abram said upset at her discontent. They have had this conversation many times over the years, and every time Abram tried to reassure her that neither he nor God is was displeased with her because she was barren... Abram pulled her close to him and once again reassured her of both God's love and his. Abram could not comfort her this time. This time she would take matters into her own hands. She would have Hagar, her servant, become a surrogate mother. Sarai convinced Abram that this was the best option for them if they were ever going to have a child. Abram tried to argue with Sarai but it was no use. Her mind was made up, and reluctantly he agreed.

Soon after the decision was made, Hagar became pregnant. She gave birth to a son. What Sarai thought would bring joy to her now caused her to be angry and jealous of Hagar. Hagar in turn looked down on Sarai. She had given Abram a son, something that Sarai could not do. The jealousy and resentment began to be like a disease, tormenting Sarai to the point of mistreating Hagar.

Abram was unaware of what Sarai was doing to torment Hagar, and she was reluctant to tell him, knowing that he would not believe her over the words of his beloved Sarai. The only choice she had was to take the child and flea into the dessert. It was better to take a chance out in the dessert than to remain in the house of Abram.

While in the dessert an Angel of the Lord appeared before Hagar and asked, "Where have you come from, and where is it that you are going?'

"I am running away from my mistress, Sarai, because she has mistreated me."

The Angel of the Lord instructed her to return to Abram's tent and dwell with his people. She was to name her son Ishmael, which means "God hears."

Some time had passed when the Lord appeared to Abram and told him that his decedents would be as many as the stars. "How is that going to happen as I am nearly one hundred and Sarai is ninety?" Abram questioned. Will this come through my son Ishmael?"

"No," said the Lord, "your wife Sarai will have a son who you will name Isaac and from this day forward you will be known as Abraham and your

wife would be called Sarah." Abraham believed what the Lord had told him. He never doubted God, but Sarah's heart and mind were filled with doubt. She knew very well that the possibility of having a child had long since passed. She and Abraham were much older now. Far too old for them to become parents.

Months had passed since the Angel of the Lord had appeared before Abraham, now Sarah was feeling even more certain that God would not fulfill his promise to Abraham through a child of their own. "God, must surely be angry with me, why else would He have brought this shame on me." Sarah whispered under her breath while she prepared the noon meal.

After Abraham finished the noon meal he decided to sit outside his tent. While sitting there he saw three men passing by, and he ran to greet them. "If I have found favor with you please wash your feet and stay awhile. I will bring you something to eat before you continue on your journey." Abraham said as he showed them to his tent. The men gladly accepted Abraham's invitation. When Abraham returned with the meal one of the men spoke...

"Where is your wife, Sarah?"

"There in the tent," he replied.

Then the Lord said to Abraham, "I will come again this time next year and you will have a son."

Sarah was standing at the entrance to the tent listening. When she heard what was said to Abraham she laughed to herself because she knew that she this was impossible. She had given up hope long ago of ever having a child.

The Lord said to Abraham, "Why did Sarah laugh, is anything to difficult for the Lord?"

Sarah opened the entrance to the tent and said, "I did not laugh," because she was afraid. "How did they know she had laughed when she had not laughed out loud, "she thought to herself, "Who are these men and how do they know my thoughts?"

The Lord looked at her and said "No? But you did laugh..."

Sarah realized that he was steadfastly certain of what she was afraid to admit—the truth. Could this be? Was she really going to have a child? A slight smile creased the corners of her mouth as she thought about what these strangers had told her husband.

It was true! With every passing day Abraham thought Sarah grew more beautiful. She even looked much younger. Soon Sarah shared the news with

Abraham. "God has blessed us, Abraham. We are going to have a child. Abraham and Sarah cried tears of joy together. God had kept His promise. Sarah was going to be a mother. Not just any mother but, the mother of a great nation. She knew that though she had doubted God, He had never left her and His promises were true. Her life would never be the same. Even though she had tried to take matters into her own hands she could not deny that God had bigger and better plans.

Sarah lifted her eyes towards heaven and laughed. It was not the same laugh as before. This time she laughed at the miraculous way in which God had chosen to reveal himself to her. (If you want to read more about Sarah and Abraham you can begin to read in the book of Genesis)

Sarah is no different from many of us. Like Sarah, we too often take matters into our own hands. We think that we know better than God. Sometimes we may even ask our husbands to do something that God has not called him to do. We must seek the Lord in all things; in matters that concern us and matters than concern our husbands. If he is to be the man God has called him to be then we must give him the respect and admiration that God has commanded us to give.

Sometimes when we think that we are doing what is in his best interest, we need to stop and ask the Lord to direct our paths. It took Sarah many years to get it right. I believe this changed the way she worked alongside Abraham. God not only was the God of Abraham and her son Isaac but He was her God too.

Digging Deeper

1. Read Ephesians 5:33 Wives are to _____
   their husbands. What are some ways you can show respect to your husband? _____

   _____

2. Read 1 Thessalonians. 5:11 and 14. What can you do today to encourage your husband? _____

   _____

3. Do others view your husband with respect based on what you say about him? Yes _____ No _____

   If you answered no let me encourage you to begin today by considering what it is you say to others about him. Read James 3:6-10 and consider the depth of your words as James warns us of the dangers of a loose tongue.

4. Answer this question honestly – Am I quick to take matters into my own hands or willing to wait on God for the answers? _____

   _____

PRAY THIS PRAYER:

Lord, I am so blessed that you have given me (you fill in his name) as my husband. Help me to show him respect. Guard my words and my actions before others where he is concerned. Give me grace towards him. Help me show him that I love him above all others. Help me Lord to wait on you and as you lead him walk with him not ahead of him. Guide his steps Lord. Keep him close and me closer so that I will be able to minister alongside him as he builds your kingdom. To God be the Glory, Amen.

Design #15

"QUEEN FOR A DAY"

Proverbs 31:25 - "Strength and dignity are her clothing, and she smiles at the future."

In today's society, strength and dignity do not seem to be very important. Strong women are seen as those who are outspoken, headstrong, and often times, very *un*dignified. She is more concerned with how she looks on the outside than what she look like on the inside.

I like to think that you are concerned with being a godly woman; after all, that is why you are reading this book; because you want to be a different kind of woman. Not just pretty on the outside but pretty on the inside.

Strength and dignity are the clothing that adorns our Proverbs 31 woman. She is the woman whose character was well known by those she came in with contact daily. We have learned that her pattern of life is one that is filled with hard work and love of family. Those with whom she socializes know her husband. He is well known and respected, in part due to the actions of his wife. Her actions are above reproach. When she walks into a room, everyone notices her, not because of her great beauty, nor because of her position in society, not even because of her abundant talent, but because she has devoted her life in the service of others and she carries herself with strength and dignity.

We do not see much of that in our society today. We are more concerned with our freedom. Self- expression is one of those freedoms. Our society praises women who are flamboyant, and our young women end up wanting to emulate these women. What we have seen is a generation of young women who are trading strength and dignity for elements of self-expression. The father of lies has cunningly worked so well in this area. Being seen as a woman of dignity is viewed as out-dated and old-fashioned.

I was watching a movie some time ago and the main character was a young woman who was trying to discover her "womanhood." She desperately wanted to discover her femininity but she did not want to be seen as "prudish." She set out to make this self-discovery over the summer and found herself in a compromising situation. This was a very **old** movie, and guess what happened. You guessed it! She decided this was not the reputation that she really wanted for herself. If we took that same movie and put a modern spin on it, she would have been laughed at for holding to these "Christian" values.

The Proverbs 31 woman is not intimidated by the moral decline of our society; rather she is encouraged by the Holy Spirit that lives within her to pursue godliness. I applaud you for choosing strength and dignity as a way of life. So dear sister, let's take a look in the closet of our heart and see what sort of things we can find in there to wear.

At the beginning of the day, not only does she wear strength and dignity but she faces the day with a smile. Can you get a mental picture of this woman in your head for a few minutes? Picture her raising her head up each morning, even before she places one foot on the floor; God has begun to reveal Himself to her. "This is the day the Lord has made," she thinks to herself and a smile comes across her face. "I will rejoice and be glad in it." She doesn't dread the activities of the day. She rejoices in them. Whatever you will face, this is a day that the Lord has made. So rejoice, be glad. Smile.

This is not always going to be easy, because there may be days that are filled with sorrow. No matter what happens, you know that your heart will be heavy with pain. That is okay. While you may not be singing and rejoicing on the outside you can still say, "Thank you Lord for THIS day, THIS moment, and THIS experience. Because I know that whatever I face today, I can face it with Your strength and dignity."

We can learn so much from the "virtuous" woman in this particular verse. I think back to those days in my own life when I really did not feel like I had much to rejoice about. Days and weeks filled with pain and sorrow that was *almost* more than I could bear. Days when the enemy had me in his jaws, and had it not been for the strength of the Lord in me I would have surely been defeated.

One of the things I love about this woman is that even though she seems too good to be true, there is always an element about her that is within the grasp of possibility.

The word *strength* comes from the Hebrew word *oz* which means; fortress, might, power and strength. It comes from the root word *azaz*, which means to be strong, to become fixed. We are to become fixed upon the Lord. He is our fortress and our tower of strength. In Psalm 18:2 the Bible tells us:

The LORD is my rock and my fortress and my deliverer,
My God, my rock, in whom I take refuge;
My shield and the horn of my salvation, my stronghold.[39]

The Lord knows that you will need to depend on His strength to make it through the day. Therefore, as we face the challenges of each new day, we are to clothe ourselves in the strength of the Lord. I wish I could tell you this is how I have lived all my life, but I cannot. I am just like you. My desire is to face each day with a renewed commitment, to put a smile on my face and dress in the strength of the Lord.

Now that she has chosen to be clothed in the strength of the Lord, she also needs a few accessories. As she looks for something to compliment her strength, she finds dignity in her closet, and of course, they are the perfect match.

Once again, I want us to look at the word and the context in which it is used here. When we read the word *dignity*, immediately we think of the formal reserve or seriousness of manner, appearance, or language of a person. I think of being in a room with the President of the United States and acting in a manner that is appropriate for the occasion. Being dignified! Here again we have to look at the Hebrew word and the context of how it is used. Here is a woman who is worthy of honor and esteem. Wow! It is important that others recognize that her immense love for the

39 New American Standard Bible

Lord causes her to live in such a way as to never bring shame and disgrace to Him (her Lord) or her family. Do you know many women in your circle of friends and family who fit this description?

Before she heads out the door, she checks herself one more time to make sure that she is appropriately dressed. She has on her strength and dignity. She began the day wearing a smile, but she takes one final look to make sure that as she faces this day, she still has on the smile that she began the day with. Sometimes we have good intentions. We wake up singing, but by the time we finish getting ourselves, and the rest of the family, out the door our smile has turned into a frown and we don't look quite as pretty anymore.

When I first met my husband he told me that what got his attention was my smile. He is always reminding me to smile. He tells me that it is my best feature. I have to work at it though. There are days when I just do not feel like smiling; however, we have seen times when someone's smile will light up a room. I want to be that kind of person.

I attended a function over the Christmas holiday in the home of one of our city's prominent families. They were hosting a brunch to raise money for a worthwhile charity. One of my friends suggested that we go. She knew the family, and had attended these functions in years past, and wanted to see their new home. When we drove up to the house, I immediately felt "out of my element." The home was 12,000 square feet of luxury. Every room was a show place. My friend and I walked around the home looking in every room, admiring its beauty. Although I am not much of a socialite, I mingled as much as possible with people that I had little in common. I knew only a few of the women there, and though I tried to fit in, I felt like a paper plate in a china cabinet.

Once I returned to my office, at the church, I told some of the staff about the house and how out of place I felt. One of the pastors said to me, "Just walk in there and smile." I was reminded that the strength of our character comes when we carry ourselves as the daughter of the King of Kings and we can smile. People may not know who you are, but they will surely notice your strength and dignity, and they cannot miss your smile. Hold you head high, even when you have to work hard at it. God has given you His strength, and you can rejoice and be glad.

Now let's see if we can find another example of a Proverbs 31 woman, this woman has a book of the Bible written about her. Esther is her name and the name of the book written about her.

King Ahasueras was in the third year of his reign as king over 127 provinces that stretched from India to Ethiopia. No one had more power than he had, and he exercised his power on a regular basis.

The King was holding a banquet in the palace for all of the nobility and attendants, officers of the armies of Persia, and Media, as well as the princes of all 127 provinces. It was a feast like no other with plenty of wine and dancing. For 180 days he displayed his royal glory and the splendor of his majesty. At the end of those days he hosted another feast for all of those who were present at the citadel of Susa, from the greatest to the least, everyone was invited to attend. At the end of the seventh day of the feast, the King commanded that the seven eunuchs who served in his court bring the Queen into the court. He wanted to "show her off."

Queen Vasti was holding a banquet herself when the servants of the king approached her.

"My lady", one of them spoke. "It would please the King if you would come to the great court."

Vashti was reclining by the pool with her ladies-in-waiting. She quickly rose to her feet, and turned to the servants of the king and spoke, "Tell his majesty the King that I will NOT parade before those drunken men again". It was not uncommon for the King to summon her. He had called for her on numerous occasions only to parade her before the gawking crowd of drunken princes and officers; He wanted to show them her great beauty. This time she was not going to go. With those words, she turned her back to them and excused them from her presence.

The eunuchs returned to the King, who was reclining in the court along with the princes of Persia and Media, and delivered Queen Vashti's words and King Ahasueras was enraged. "How dare she refuse me!" Does she not know that I am the king and whatever I command is to be obeyed? According to the law what is to be done with her for refusing me?" he asked those closest to him. The words were out of his mouth before he realized the impact they would have on Vashti.

The men sitting closest to the king began to discuss the queen's refusal. They said, "She has not only disgraced the king; but all the women in the kingdom will surely hear of her actions, and they in turn will treat their husbands in like manner, bringing contempt upon their husbands"

"What then must I do?" Pounding his fist upon the table the king commanded, "I cannot let this action go unpunished."

"Your majesty should issue an edict that Queen Vashti will no longer be allowed in your presence and that her royal position will be given to another," replied the king's advisors. "This way all the women of Persia will know that you cannot refuse your master."

The king was so angry that he immediately called for his scribes to write such an edict, and he put his seal upon it. The edict was sent to all the provinces in his kingdom. The queen was removed from the palace and would never be allowed to visit the king again.

Some time passed and the King began thinking back over the actions that had led him to make such a command. He decided it was time to seek a new queen.

"Gather up all the beautiful young virgins in the kingdom, bring them to the palace and bring those who are fit for a king to me!" he told Heigi, one of the eunuchs. So, the process of selecting a replacement for Vashti began.

There was a Jewish man in Susa named Mordecai who had been taken into exile from Jerusalem during the reign of King Nebuchadnezzar. He was raising his niece, Esther, who was exquisitely beautiful. Mordecai, upon hearing that the king was looking for a new queen, rushed to tell Esther of the news.

"Esther, the King has taken all of the beautiful, young virgins into the palace in search of a queen. You will surely be taken as well. When that happens, you must not tell them that you are Jewish. It is very important that they do not know." Esther agreed to keep her identity a secret. It was not long until Esther was noticed for her beauty and just as Mordecai had predicted she was taken to the palace.

Hegai, who was in charge of all the women brought into the palace, was so captivated by her beauty that he provided her with the finest cosmetics and clothes that the palace had to offer. Nothing was denied her. For twelve months, Esther remained in the king's harem being groomed and counseled, as required, before she would be presented to the king. Each day her Uncle Mordecai would walk to the palace to learn how Esther was doing.

"Hegai, I have done all that you have asked of me. What will become of me now that I have fulfilled my time of beautification?" Esther asked as she put her hands on Hegai's hands. Hegai had grown very fond of this women,

and he gave her wise counsel on what she would do, and say, when she was presented to the King.

When the time came for her to go before the king, Esther followed Hegai's instructions and asked for only that which Hegai had instructed. The moment Esther walked into the king's court he was captivated by her beauty and he immediately fell in love with her. "Come and sit with me.," the king said, speaking softly so that she would feel at ease in his presence. They sat and talked until the morning dawned. He then decided that he would make her his Queen.

It was a grand wedding like nothing the kingdom had seen before. Even that of Queen Vashti could not compare to this, nor could Vashti's beauty compare to Esther's. Esther kept her identity a secret from the king, because she had promised her uncle that she would not tell the King.

Time pass, and Mordecai would come to the palace gates every day where he would see Esther walking in the gardens. Their eyes would meet for a moment but they never spoke a word to each other. Esther longed to bring her uncle into the palace to live, but she honored him, and would not make her Jewish heritage known for fear it would not go well with Mordecai.

One evening while he was sitting at the gates Mordecai heard of a plot against the king by one of his own counsel. He knew that he would be risking everything, but he had to get word to Esther. As night fell, he made his way to the gates of the palace where he saw Esther walking in the garden accompanied by several maidservants. Mordecai called to her quietly through the palace gates, doing his best not to draw attention to himself.

"Esther", he called to her. Hearing her name, she turned to catch a glimpse of her Uncle behind the palace wall near the gate at the entrance. Not wanting anyone to notice him, she moved slowly towards the gate where he was standing.

"What are you doing here, Uncle? You mustn't let the king's guards see you," she said as she touched his weathered hands. "It is good to see you. How I have missed you."

"Esther, my dear child, I have news that I must tell you." With those words, he began to share with Esther what he had heard in the courtyard of the palace.

Esther nodded in understanding, and returned to the garden where she had been just moments earlier. That night in her room, Esther prayed about how she would tell the King of such a plot. She could not just go into the king's presence and blurt out what she had been told. Somehow, she **must** *get word to him. Because the King loved Esther, when she requested an audience with him, he usually granted her request. She told King Ahasuerus of the plot and of the Jewish man named Mordecai who had given her this valuable information. But, she did not tell him that Mordecai was her uncle.*

The King investigated the matter, found it to be true, and had the men responsible hung. Later he promoted a man named Haman to the highest-ranking official in the land. Haman's position went to his head and his heart was filled with pride. All of the king's servants were required to bow and pay homage to Haman. But Mordecai refused. When questioned as to why his answer was "I am a Jew." This made Haman so angry that he wanted Mordecai dead. Haman's hatred grew so much that he wanted to eliminate all of the Jews in the kingdom. In order to fulfill this desire to kill Mordecai Haman knew he must first get the king's blessing.

"Your Majesty, there is a group of people, the Jews who were exiled into this country, who do not fear the king. In fact, they mock the king. They don't fit in, and they disregard your laws and commands. If it pleases they king I would like to be your servant in ridding the kingdom of these worms" Haman shouted as he knelt before King Ahasuerus. "I will even help to pay for the operation myself," he boasted.

The king was overcome with anger. Under the influence of too much wine and poor judgment he took off his signet ring and handed it to Haman. "It is your money, do what you want with it."

Haman instructed his servants to draw up the document and put the king's seal on it. He instructed them to distribute the document throughout all of the king's provinces. The Jews were gathered up and Haman had begun to have them killed.

When Mordecai learned about what was being done to the Jews, he got word to Esther, and she was distraught over the fate of her people. Determined to do something Esther began to pray. She instructed Mordecai to do the same. Esther knew that she could not confront the king. If she approached the king without an invitation, she could be killed. She dressed in her finest clothes and waited in front of the king's court. For three days, she waited and as she was walking past the open door to the throne room, he saw her. The king had never seen her look more beautiful...

He motioned for her to come in. "Esther, why have you come? What it is that you want? Ask of me anything unto the half of my kingdom and I will give it to you."

Esther chose her words carefully. Her very own life was at stake, for she too was a Jew. If the King and Haman found out she would surely die. She bowed before the King and asked that he attend a dinner party in his honor and "by all means bring your faithful servant Haman."

The king summoned Haman, "The Queen is holding a dinner this evening in my honor, and she was invited you to attend." Haman, feeling very proud of himself, accepted the invitation. As they were dining at the table of the queen, King Ahasuerus asked her again, "What do you want?"

Esther closed her eyes and took a deep breath, "This is what I want," she said. "If you are pleased with me then I would like for you to come and dine with me again tomorrow, both of you, then I will tell you." The king was amused, and because of his love for the queen was willing to go along with the game.

As Haman left the queens table he was feeling very proud of himself. As he was walking past the palace gate he saw Mordecai sitting there. "How dare he!" he thought. He was determined that this was not going to ruin his night. He continued on his way home. After arriving at home, he told his wife of the night's events, and how he had seen Mordecai sitting at the palace gates. The more he talked about it the more enraged he became. How was it that the one man he wanted dead was still alive. As he was ranting, his wife suggested building a gallows, then order Mordecai hung right there in the courtyard of the palace. This would eliminate his problem and hers. She was tired of hearing about Mordecai. He could continue to party and be merry with the King and Queen, and she would never have to hear about it again. Haman thought it was a wonderful idea.

That night the king was restless so he decided to look over the written logs of the daily events that had taken place over the past few months when he came across an entry. It was when Esther had told him of a plot to kill him that had been discovered by a man named Mordecai. The king got up the next day he asked, "Has anything been done to thank Mordecai for saving my life." Much to his surprise the answer was no. The king called Haman into the great hall, "Haman, if a man honors the King and saves his life what sort of honor should be bestowed on him." Haman was sure that the king was talking about him so he offered a suggestion, "Your Majesty, if any man has done such a thing he should be treated as if he was the son of the king." Haman had no idea that the king was talking about Mordecai.

The king said to Haman, "Take quickly the robes and horses and find Mordecai and do just as you have said. Be sure that you follow the instructions to the letter!"

Mordecai was paraded through the gates and into the Palace courtyard like royalty with Haman leading the way. This time it was Mordecai that was given honor, not Haman. He was furious!

That evening Haman was angry and upset, but when he was summoned to dine with the Queen Esther, he could not refuse. As they were dining, Esther looked into the eyes of the king and said, "I am ready to tell you my request." The king took her hand and kissed it. Again he told her, "You can have half of my kingdom if you so desire."

"Your Majesty, bowing her head, she began choosing her next words very carefully, "It is my life and the life of my people that I desire. My people are to be sold into slavery and killed, completely wiped out! I would have remained quiet had this been just an annoyance to the king".

Taking her face in his hands, he pulled her chin up and asked, "Who has done this?" Esther spoke as she looked directly at Haman, "A man who is an enemy of the king," and she pointed to Haman.

The king ordered that Haman be hung on the very gallows that he had built for Mordecai. Esther asked the king to allow her to bring Mordecai into the king's court to become one of the king's faithful servants and it was done.

I realize that this story was much longer than the previous ones, but it is a story that the God devoted an entire book of the Bible to. I felt that we needed to see how the Lord worked in Esther's life from the beginning of the story to the end. Some stories of women in the Bible are told with the lines of a few verses. However, there are only two women that God devoted an entire book to, Ruth and Esther. I hope that after reading this story, you are familiar with Esther. Perhaps you had never really thought about what her life must have been like. She undoubtedly was a beautiful woman inside and out. She was clothed in strength and dignity. Her faith in God sustained her and gave her wisdom when she needed it the most. As a young foreign orphan, she had no idea that she one day she would become a queen. That thought never occurred to her until the day she was summoned by the king. Well, you too have been summoned by the king, the King of Kings. You are called to be set apart for His glory. His purpose for your life is better than anything that you could dream up. Look at Esther, this was certainly better than any dream she could have had.

Digging Deeper:

1. Read the following verses on strength, Deut.31:6, Psalm 28:8 and Isa. 12:2 Where does your strength come from?_____.
    Are you dressed with His strength?

2. Read Job 40:10 What are we to cloth ourselves in? _____
    _____

3. The Hebrew word for dignity is *hadar*, which means honor, majesty and splendor. Read 1 Kings 3:13

    "In addition I will give you what you did not ask for, _____
    and _____.

4. Read 1 Tim. 2:1-7. There is a purpose found in this passage and it is the reason we are to clothe ourselves in the strength and dignity of the Lord. What is that purpose (vs.4)? _____
    _____

Pray this Prayer:

This is a day the Lord has made and I WILL REJOICE and be GLAD in it. Lord, you have made me in your image and you have not created anything that is not beautiful. Help me Lord to cloth myself in strength and dignity and to put a smile on my face every day, even in the midst to pain and sorrow let me rejoice in knowing you.

Design #16
"HOLD YOUR TONGUE"

Proverbs 31: 26 - She opens her mouth in wisdom,
and the teaching of kindness is on her tongue.

I wish I could say that every time I opened my mouth words of wisdom flowed and kindness is all I ever speak, but truthfully, I can't. I am sure that most, if not all, of you are just like me in admitting your shortcomings when it comes to your speech. So how is it that we could possibly ever live up to this passage of scripture?

For the past several months life has been exceedingly difficult. Many things have taken place that have made me "open my mouth." What is it that we need to understand about this passage? The "virtuous" woman will carefully choose her words. When she opens her mouth, it is for a reason; and when she speaks, she speaks wisdom. The Greek word for wisdom in this verse is the word *chokmah,* which means: skillful or prudent in religious affairs, ethical.

Once again we are going to unpack this passage and glean as much truth from it as we can, leaning directly upon the scriptures for our understanding.

King Lemuel's mother must have been a very prudent, wise woman. For her to direct her son to be looking for a woman who possessed these qualities, requires a mother who has gained some wisdom of her own.

I have a son, who is single now. If I could hand pick a woman for him what sort of woman would I choose? Well, I would look for a young woman who was well on her way to possessing these qualities. What mother would not want this type of young woman for a daughter-in-law? While I would love to find a rare jewel with all of these qualities, I think that for most of us would be happy to have a young woman who passionately sought to possess these qualities herself.

I dare say that at age 21, I wasn't anywhere close to having possessed even a few of these qualities. Philippians 1:6 has become my life's verse, "He who began a good work in you will perfect it until the day of Christ Jesus." In other words, we are a work in progress. If we had reached perfection, there would be nothing left for God to do in our lives, and He would call us home. For that reason, He has given us instructions on how we are to pursue life in Christ Jesus.

Did you know that *wisdom* in mentioned 216 times in the Bible? The book of Proverbs alone mentions wisdom 48 times. Solomon knew the benefits to gaining wisdom. When the Lord asked him what he wanted above all things, he said **wisdom**.

What does wisdom do for us? Again, let's take a look at scripture for the answer. The Psalmist wrote in Psalm 49:3 *"My mouth will speak wisdom, And the meditation of my heart will be understanding.*

Our instruction here in Proverbs 31 is that when we do open our mouths then we are to speak with the voice of truth. We are to know when to speak and when to be silent. In Ecclesiastes, the author told his congregation (he was known as the preacher) that there is a time to speak, and a time to refrain from speaking. Not every situation requires that we share our opinion.

I have always been a talker, ever since I was a little girl. It has gotten me into more trouble than anything else in my life has. My parents were even so bold as to record my love of speech through home movies, and at the age of six they made a movie of me at Christmas. The video was made using a video camera that could not pick up sound (this was back in the 60's). You could not tell what I was saying, but you knew I was talking because my mouth was moving ninety to nothing. My parents would drag out the video and show it to all their friends, all their family, all my friends, all my potential friends, all my not so potential friends, and anyone who was within a five-mile radius of our home. (I think they still have it and would get it out and play it if they had a projector that worked.) They laughed at my expense. For years I laughed along with them, I knew why they thought it was funny, but to a young teenage girl it was anything but funny. This is how God had made me. My father went so far, in his own loving way, to try to help me overcome my love of the spoken word, *and in particular my own.* He was a bi-vocational minister of youth and music and, of course, I was one of the youth under his leadership. I will never forget the time, when I was about fourteen years old; we were going to be having a big youth fellowship after church. Before we left home that evening, my father pulled me aside and counseled me on my "problem" of always wanting to be the center of attention. He told me that whenever he thought I was trying to be the center of attention he was going to tug on his ear lobe. That was my signal to blend into the crowd and quit drawing attention to myself. My father meant well but I was wounded.

By the time the youth fellowship had started, I had forgotten about what my father and I had discussed just a few hours earlier. I was comfortably engaging in conversation with some friends, laughing and cutting up, telling silly jokes and making people laugh. I happened to look over at my father, and he reached up and tugged on his earlobe. Immediately I withdrew into a cocoon afraid to utter a single word the rest of the night. That stayed with me for years, but the need to express myself has never left me. It has been somewhat of a curse at times because in my insecurities and my need for acceptance, I have often felt that the way to gain that acceptance was to be the eloquent spokesperson filled with wisdom. I searched for ways to speak often without even being asked.

As much as I hate to admit it, I know that even this week I have said some things without putting much thought into what I have said. Just as there have been times like that, there have also been opportunities this week for me to give real encouragement to those who were in desperate need of it. I have talked with women who needed to hear that God would use the battles they are facing to shape them into the person He wants them to become. As God directed my words, I was able to point out the things that will give them hope when everything around them seems hopeless. God, in His infinite wisdom, has allowed me to walk before them and experience the things they are now facing so that I would be able to encourage them from a place I knew well. It is my belief that God never wastes pain on His children. If we will be still and open our mouths when and only when we need to, God can and will use us in ways we never thought possible.

I can tell you from personal experience that I have not followed this principle of "being quiet" especially when it comes to my children. For some reason, (God only knows why) mothers feel we must impart truth upon our children at any cost and they must listen to what we say. The Bible is clear about the benefits of wisdom and instruction. The two share center stage in many passages in Proverbs. Proverbs 1:8 tells us to hear our father's instructions and give heed to our mother's sayings. These are beneficial to those who will do this. Proverbs 1:20, 33 says, "Wisdom shouts in the streets; a fool despises knowledge; and he who listens will live securely and will be at ease from the dread of evil" (Pam's paraphrase). There is a time to be still and quiet and let God do what only He can, especially after you have done all He has commanded you to do as a parent. So hard! So hard! There is nothing more painful to a Christian parent than to see your child turn their back on the truth you taught them. We want to impart wisdom upon them at any cost. Unfortunately, it may cost you a relationship with that child. Therefore, we need to exercise wisdom and discernment when we feel the need to give wisdom to children, especially our adult children.

On numerous occasions, I have felt compelled to "preach" truth only to feel frustrated and upset because my children did not see things my way. They can tell when I am getting "preachy", because in the past they have made remarks about mom "preaching" at them. They know. They know when you are preaching and when you are showing love. There definitely is a difference. 1 Corinthians 13: 1 reads like this in the Message translation: *"If I speak with human eloquence and angelic ecstasy but don't love, I'm nothing but the creaking of a rusty gate."*[40] Your family and friends know when the words you speak are spoken with love, and when you are just speaking with human eloquence.

God warns us in James chapter three about opening our mouths to speak. I would encourage you to stop right here and read that chapter. If you have several versions of the Bible, read it in each of them. After studying this, here is what I believe the warning is for those of us who feel the need to speak.

---

40 The Message Bible

Be careful what you say: because when you say it, you will never be able to take it back and relive that moment again. No one is perfect, you are going to make mistakes and say things you wish you had not, but understand that in order to bridle or harness the spoken word you MUST use wisdom.

Some time ago when speaking with my son I began to feel a sense of urgency about letting him know who he was in Christ, and that there is coming a day of judgment for all those who are outside of Christ. It wasn't a hell-fire sort of speech, but I felt myself being drawn into an unwanted conversation so I quickly removed myself from the temptation to give him one of my many prepared "come to Jesus" talks. He asked me if I was going to have another one of "those" conversations and I just replied, "No we are not". To which he replied "why not". He was expecting it, so I stopped after we hung up the phone and said a quick prayer. "Lord, bring him home." A prayer my friend taught me to pray. He had no idea that I prayed that for him, but God does and one day he will find his way home, of that, I am sure.

The second part of the verse 26 reminds us that when we do feel compelled to "open our mouth" we are to do so teaching kindness. Many times those of us who profess to be Christians are anything but kind. I learned years ago when I was first introduced to the ministry that Christians can be anything but kind. I have a saying: "Christians will shoot their wounded and eat their young" I don't think that originated with me but I have added another part to that saying: "then they will boast that it is done in the name of the Lord." We often find ourselves caught up in trying to be spiritual, and we are vicious and unkind to our brothers and sisters in Christ. We will see or hear something that we believe is out of the will of God, and because He has appointed us guardians of the truth, we feel justified in our "necessity" to rebuke them. I knew of someone who believed they had the "gift of rebuke". Paul in his letter to the Galatians wrote: "But if you bite and devour one another, take care that you are not consumed by one another." What you say may come back on you. He goes on to write the flesh will set its desires against the Spirit. We are to walk in a manner that is worthy of the calling of Christ. One of the fruits of living in the Spirit is kindness.

As we grow in Christ, we are being made perfect in His likeness. We do not just wake up one day having wisdom on our lips and kindness in our hearts. We wake up every morning with a choice. Will I bridle my tongue today and speak only kindness? Will I be careful to open my mouth only when it is to speak truth, even if it hurts, not to be vicious, but to bring hope, and healing to those who need to hear? Our prayer should be to speak words that encourage and lift up my brothers and sisters in Christ. This should be our prayer...

I have chosen Elizabeth from the book of Luke, to spotlight in this chapter, because, as we will, see she has spoken words of wisdom. She is the mother of John the Baptist

It was a hot day as Mary sat pondering what the Angel of the Lord had told her: "You are going to be the mother of the Son of God." A smile crossed Mary's face as she twisted a blade of grass in her fingers. She thought once again, on the words, "You have found favor with God". Thinking back to that moment once again, Mary meditated on her own words, "How is this going to be possible?" Again, she smiled as she remembered what the angel told her about her cousin Elizabeth: she too was going to have a baby, for nothing was impossible with God! Mary could only imagine how thrilled Elizabeth and Zacharias must be. They had been married for years and had never able to have a child.

Mary did not doubt the words of the angel, but her mind was flooded with thoughts and emotions. If anyone could understand what was going on in her heart and mind, she felt that Elizabeth could. At that moment, Mary decided that it would be a good time to visit her cousin Elizabeth who lived in the hill country. Mary stood up and made her way home to ask permission from her family to make the journey to city in Judah to visit her cousin Elizabeth. There was not time to waste it was important that she leave at once so she could arrive before it got dark.

Elizabeth was now in her sixth month of pregnancy, she was now in seclusion until the birth of her child. It has been six months since Zacharias had spoken any words to Elizabeth, but they managed to communicate with one another through a writing tablet. Although she loved Zacharias, she longed for some company, especially another woman, with whom she could share her joy. Someone she could laugh with, and someone who understood what she was feeling— the inexpressible joy of being mother after all these years. She was so thankful that God had found favor with her, but six months was a long time for silence.

Elizabeth was sitting at the table in her kitchen kneading some dough to make bread when she felt the baby kick. She thought to herself, "You will be a strong boy, I'm sure of it; no girl would kick as hard as you my little one." Elizabeth placed her hand on her ever growing stomach and marveled at the fact that she was finally going to be a mother.

She rose and placing the dough on a board, set it near the window so the heat of the sun would help it to rise quickly. She had not been moving quick enough these days, and she was afraid that Zacharias would not have any bread for the evening meal, if God did not help the loaf of bread rise quickly. She uttered a prayer of thanksgiving for God's goodness " Lord, if you have found favor with me, and having seen fit to bless me with a child, could You please cause this bread to rise in time for dinner? I know that nothing is impossible for You. Amen!" Elizabeth smiled as she dusted the flour from her dress. Looking out the window Elizabeth noticed a young woman walking towards the house who looked familiar. She was a little too far away to recognize, so Elizabeth decided to go out to meet her. As they drew closer to each other Elizabeth recognized the young woman, it was her cousin Mary. Mary called out to Elizabeth and the baby she was carrying seemed to leap for joy at the sound of her voice. The two women embraced and Elizabeth took Mary by the hand. As she led her back to the house she asked, "What on earth has brought you here?

"I have some news," Mary said, as they walked back towards the house, "I too am going to have a baby."

Elizabeth, suddenly filled with the Holy Spirit, turned and spoke to Mary, "Mary, blessed are you among women, and blessed is the child you are carrying. Why has the mother of the Lord come to visit me? The moment I heard the sound of your voice the child I am carrying jumped in my womb."

Mary took Elizabeth's hands and shared the story of how the angel of the Lord had appeared to her, and told her that she would conceive and give birth to the Son of God. Elizabeth wiped the tears from her eyes, pulled Mary close to her, and hugged her tightly.

For years, Elizabeth had heard Zacharias teach of a coming Messiah that would be born of a virgin. Not until today did Elizabeth believe that she would be a witness to the fulfillment of this prophesy.

"Mary, God has found great favor with you, and you will be blessed for having believed what the Lord has spoken to you. God has seen fit to bestow on

both of us His goodness. Who would have believed that I would have a child when I am well past my years of giving birth, yet look," she told Mary as she placed her hands on her stomach. "God has plans for your child and for mine. We are both experiencing the miracle of birth, but you Mary, are carrying the Holy One."

Mary thought about what Elizabeth had said. God had found favor with her. What she had done to deserve His favor? She didn't know, but she would have time to think about it. She decided that she would stay with Elizabeth until she gave birth.

The two women became giddy with excitement and Elizabeth could not wait for Zacharias to return home. She didn't care whether the bread rose or not and she felt it wouldn't matter to Zacharias once he heard Mary's news.

It would have been easy for Elizabeth to think nothing of a kick from her unborn child when Mary first greeted her. At six months along, surely it wasn't the first time this had happened. Since she had experienced a miracle from God in her own life, every kick was a sign of the blessings from the Lord. However, because she was keenly aware of God's presence and was listening to His voice, the Holy Spirit revealed something magnificent to her.

It was then that she spoke. She did not jump to conclusions about Mary's condition. She did not ask a million questions or try to analyze the situation. Instead, she waited on the Lord to give her the right words to speak. God spoke wisdom through her to bring comfort to Mary. Try to put yourself in Mary's position. What would help you to come to terms with what you had experienced? Sometimes we need the wisdom of a godly person to speak truth to us and confirm what we ourselves already know.

The angel of the Lord did not tell Mary "Go to your cousin Elizabeth and she will confirm for you what I have just told you." Mary, thinking about what she had been told, was prompted by the Holy Spirit to go visit Elizabeth. God knew Elizabeth would speak words of wisdom and reassurance to Mary about what was taking place in her life.

When we walk in the Spirit of God, He will use us to minister in a variety of way I would have never thought that God could use the messed up life I had lived to help someone else, but He did, and He continues to. There is nothing that you and I will encounter that God does not know about it long before it happens. He knows what experiences we will have.

When we are walking in the Spirit, He will use the events in our lives in ways we could never have dreamed.

Don't think that God cannot use our suffering and negative experiences for His glory. Even when those experiences that are a result of walking outside of God's will, they can still be used to praise His name when we allow Him to speak through us. I cannot tell you how many people I have talked to about the pain of divorce. Had I not gone through that myself, I would not have been able to help them walk through similar circumstances. As crazy as it may sound, God continues to use my painful past to help others work through whatever it is they are facing.

When we are being used by God this way it is very important to be discerning about when to speak and what to speak. Sometimes we just have to be quiet and wait on the Holy Spirit to speak wisdom through us. For the times when we have to act quickly, that is when Holy Spirit will take over when we ask for His guidance.

DIGGING DEEPER

1. Am I willing to allow God to use the circumstances of my life to minister to someone else? Yes _____ No _____ If you answered no, why? _____

   _____

2. Ask yourself, am I speaking truth in love when faced with difficult circumstances? Read Zech 8:16 and Eph 4:15.

3. Read Job 33:3-- Where are your words to come from? _____

   _____

4. Am I asking God for discernment and wisdom when I speak? Read 1 Cor. 2:17- Write it here. _____

   _____

5. Think of a time when God used something in your life to minister to someone else and write that here. _____

_____

Pray this Prayer:

Lord, I know that you are able to do exceedingly abundantly beyond all that I could ask. I know that you desire to use my life to bring honor and glory to You. Help me to know when I need to speak truth in love, and when to be quiet. Help me to discern the truth and to speak wisdom whenever you place opportunities before me.

Design #17

"What Ever Happened To Wonder Woman"

Proverbs 31:27 --She looks well to the ways of her household. And does not eat the bread of idleness.

A few years ago at one of our women's ministry summer conferences, I led a session that I titled "What Ever Happened to Wonder Woman?" My session was about helping women balance the things in their lives. In this chapter I am going to focus on some of the things I shared at this conference.

Does your life look something like this?

5:30 a.m. - The alarm goes off and you get out of bed. You hit the treadmill, and get in a quick run or walk in before anyone in the house is up.

6:00 a.m. - It's time to spend a few minutes with the Lord.

6:15 a.m. - Your husband wakes up to the smell of coffee, and your quiet time was reduced to 15 minutes. You really wanted more time, but life has begun.

6:30 a.m. - You finish your English muffin, grab your clothes, and get the children up (if you have children) fix their breakfast, and get them dressed for school.

6:45 a.m. - You give last minute instructions then jump in the shower yourself; or maybe you had to get your shower the night before, due to the fact that your children cannot be left alone because they will kill each other.

7:00 a.m. - It is time to fix lunches for you, your husband, and the children. You consider just letting them buy their lunch this once to save time.

7:15 a.m. - You put the finishing touches on your hair and make-up. Kiss the children good-bye and hurry them out the door so they do not miss the bus, all the while brushing your teeth and putting on your shoes.

7:25 a.m. - You make the bed, put the dishes in the dishwasher, then put a load of clothes on to wash.

7:35 a.m. - You are out the door and into the mad, mad, mad rush-hour traffic.

7:40 a.m.- You are caught by the train so you wait, grumbling about the train which is keeping you from getting to work 15 minutes ahead of your boss.

7:50 a.m. – You arrive at work and start up the computer, and never look back.

5:00 p.m.- Finally you can stop work, but now you have to get little Suzie to piano lessons and Johnny to ball practice, or ballet, cheerleading, gymnastics, flute, violin, baseball, basketball, soccer or football, or maybe **all** of the above.

5:30 p.m. - You run through the grocery store just long enough to pick up a few things for supper before you pick up the kids from their various activities.

6:00 p.m. - You get the kids started on homework, and you unload the dishwasher, put the clothes in the dryer and start supper.

6:45 p.m. – If you are lucky, your family will all sit down to dinner. If you are like many families with teenagers, you will have to serve dinner in shifts.

7:00 p.m.– Now it is time to go to a ball game or a dance recital, or some other extracurricular activity that the kids are involved in, so you hop in the car the head out again. If your children are grown, you have moved into a new phase of your life, and you have been asked to be on some committee at church that is having a meeting. Maybe the grandchildren have called and you need to go to their ball game, etc. etc. etc.

8:00 p.m. - If your children are young, you have fed them bathed them and tucked them into bed. You decide to take a walk around the block, work outside in your yard until dark, do laundry; clean bathrooms or whatever else needs to be done.

9:30 p.m. - Ordinarily by this time the ball game or dance recital has ended and you hurry home to get the kids in bed. Maybe you have just spent the last hour, reading bedtime stories, getting baths, and cleaning up the supper dishes. Finally, you are ready to go sit down.

9:45 p.m. - You decide to read through your emails, and take time to answer some of them.

10:00 p.m.- You finally get to watch the news.

10:30 p.m. – You collapse into bed only to sleep with a recording of tomorrows tasks playing in your mind. What did I forget to do? You cannot sleep so you get up and jot down a few reminders, heaven forbid if you forget. It is now 12:00 midnight, and you finally drop off to sleep.

Whew!!!! Does any of this sound familiar to you? It does to me. No two days are the same; each one is filled to the max with "things to do." When life is out of balance, everything is affected by it– our body, our mind and our spirit. Let's face it most of us think we have to be "Wonder Woman." We may hold down a 40-50 hour a week job, raise 2.5 kids (and a husband); shuttle the family to every ball game, tennis lesson, and dance practice. Not to mention, serving on multiple committees, join the PTA and act as home-room mom, teach a small group, lead a bible study, prepare the meals, (or at least drive through McDonald's and get a "Happy Meal"), launder the clothes, clean the house, and work at keeping that "Barbie Doll" figure of ours. We **are** "Wonder Woman" or at least we deserve the title.

In our efforts to claim the title what we really have done is neglect ourselves. When the body is out of balance, it affects every aspect of our daily lives. Recently I had a physical injury. I was skiing in Colorado, fell, and broke my arm and shoulder. I didn't know it at the time, and I continued to ski despite the pain. My body was telling me all the while that something was wrong. For a week, I continued to try to function normally with a broken arm and shoulder. Not only I was losing sleep but also I was not allowing my body the rest it needed to heal properly. When I returned home from my trip, I was exhausted, from not only skiing, but my body was trying to heal a broken arm. I kept the healing process from going forward, because I was not taking care of myself.

God created us with a unique way of rejuvenating our cell structures so that when we get enough rest and the proper nutrients in our body, we are able to function day in and day out without burning out physically.

In the beginning, God set in order that man should rest. We read in Genesis 2:1-3 "Heaven and Earth were finished, down to the last detail. By the seventh day, God had finished his work. On the seventh day He *rested* from all His work. God blessed the seventh day. He made it a Holy Day, because on that day He rested from His work, all the creating God had done. He commanded that we should have a day of rest."[41]

In our American culture, we tend to burn the candle and both ends. Though we may say that men are the ones who typically do this, studies have been done that show women are not sleeping well, spending less time with family and friends, are too tired for sex and often drive to work drowsy, and are late for work. Working women aren't the only ones either, 74% of stay-at-home moms don't get enough sleep. In the hour before they go to bed, they are busy doing last minute chores, or getting children ready for bed and school the next day.

Not only are we not getting enough sleep but our diet has suffered too. We eat on the run and we rarely have time to sit down to dinner with the family. When we do, we have to gobble it down because we don't have enough time in the day. Every moment is committed to some activity.

There was a commercial just recently on TV for KFC. They are claiming to have the "sit-down dinner" The commercial shows a mother

---

41 Peterson, E. H. 2003. *The Message: The Bible in contemporary language.* NavPress: Colorado Springs, Colo

calling her family down to dinner. Instead of gathering at the dinner table, they run and jump in the car. Of course, you see the family pleasantly surprised when they see the mother setting KFC out on the dinner table. It is funny but so true. This is the society we live in. How many of you growing up had all of your evening meals together? How many days of the week does your family sit down at the dinner table together? If you are fortunate enough to enjoy your meals together, how many of those are fast- food meals?

I can tell you that when my children were young I cooked almost every evening meal we had. I tried to get the family to sit down together. It was not that hard when they were young, but as they grew older and their activities increased we had fewer and fewer meals at home, and more meals at the ballpark, or we would run through McDonald's and grab something. No one was home at the same time, and I was always going to something with them in the evening. Our car was the dining room. We ate while going down the road. The sad thing is now that my children are grown, I rarely cook at all. Jim will call and ask if I want to grab a bite in town. Of course, I would rather not have to go home and try to figure out what to cook so I take him up on the offer. Trying to find something healthy to eat is like trying to find a needle in a haystack—nearly impossible. It is a vicious cycle and a pattern that we have to consciously work at.

The "secret" to maintaining good health is combining a healthy eating plan with daily physical activity. While it may seem easy to follow the latest fad diet or trend going around, many of these plans excessively restrict your intake of foods or entire food groups, which can lead to inadequacies in key nutrients. "Diets" can also be hard to stick to for longer than a few weeks. Many people simply revert to their old eating habits in the end. You have to eliminate the excuses; it will be hard to maintain a healthy lifestyle if you do not. You can develop a good diet by realistically adding foods that you like. When I eat out, I try to find something that is relatively healthy and limit my portion sizes. If the restaurant does not have smaller portions and you know that you are not going to eat all of it ask the waiter to go ahead and bring you a take home box. Put half of your meal in the box right away. This will help to prevent over-eating. I am not perfect, and I wish I could say I was as slender as I wanted to be. The fact is, as I have gotten older, my metabolism has slowed down, and it is harder to maintain my weight. These are merely suggestions to help you along the way. Find what works for you.

Not only are we to take care of our physical body, but we have to take care of our inner body, which has two parts the soul, and the spirit.

The soul is that which encompasses our mind, our will and our emotion. In other words, what we do, what we think and how we feel. Let's face it we are very emotional creatures.

When we tend to take on too many commitments, our homes turn into battlefields and our marriages suffer neglect, becoming less and less exciting. We have turned into the Wicked Witch and left our family wishing we would become Sleeping Beauty, so they can rest from our constant nagging. Clean up your room. Eat your vegetables. Wash your hands after you use the bathroom. Take out the trash. How much did you spend on your golf game? You did what! If, I have told you once, I have told you a thousand times, chew with your mouth closed. Keep your hands to yourself. I wish you would learn to pick up after yourself. I am really sick and tired of.... Does any of this sound familiar? Our heart and our emotions cry out "Lord, could I just have 5 minutes of peace in the bathroom without someone wanting to know WHAT I AM DOING IN HERE?"

Our emotions cry out for peace. John 14:27 says "Peace I leave you, my peace I give, not as the world gives. Do not let you hearts be troubled, neither let them be afraid.

One thing that affects that peace in our soul is over-commitment. Over-commitment affects our family relationships. When we are over-committed, our families pay a high price, especially, when everyone else's needs come before theirs. We do this unintentionally when we cannot say no. We feel that we can handle all of it. We are Wonder Women after all. Many times, we will take on too much out of a sense of obligation. I am very bad at that, I must admit. I think I need to do whatever I am asked to do. Not long ago, things in the office were very hectic and my boss and I were talking when he said to me, "You know you don't wear a cape?" I thought surely he much be mistaken, didn't he see my cape? My response was "I want to be all things to all people." I did not want to admit that I could not do it all. It was not in my nature to do that. We want to be indispensable, at home, at work, at church, wherever we are. Some women are worse than others are when it comes to this. Our emotional side tells us a few things when this happens. First, we feel that people expect us to do it, and we are failures to God if we do not. Secondly, people will not understand if we say no. Thirdly, we do not want to disappoint them. On and on we go. We can burn out very quickly. Peace becomes something we, only read about, but never experience.

God wants us to live in peace. He has devoted more than 200 verses in the Bible to peace. Here are a few of them for you to take with you:

- **Proverbs 17:1**- A meal of bread and water in contented peace is better than a banquet spiced with quarrels.
- **Psalm 133:1** - How wonderful, how beautiful, when brothers and sisters get along! It's like costly anointing oil flowing down head and beard,
- **Psalm 29:11**- GOD makes his people strong. GOD gives his people peace.
- **Proverbs 17: 1**- Better a dry crust with peace and quiet, than a house full of feasting and strife.
- **Isaiah 26:3**- You will keep in perfect peace him whose mind is steadfast because he trusts in You.
- **Proverbs 14:30** - A heart of peace gives life to the body, but envy rots the bones.

The Greek word for peace means the absence of war or conflict. Wouldn't you like to have peace in your home?

Our soul is where our emotions live. That is why we are able to experience joy and sorrow, pain and pleasure, contentment and unrest, love and hate. All of those emotions come from what is in our heart and soul.

Several things can rob us of peace. Worry, anxiety, fear, anger, self-pity and remorse. We are the emotional creatures, and as such, we can spend a lot of time and energy on these emotions, and complain that we do not have time to cultivate spiritual disciplines like Bible Study, prayer, worship and fellowship. When we spend our time on the negative emotions, then our nerves become frazzled and our bodies ache and our relationships are strained.

What is the cure? Trading worry for meditation, anxiety for prayer, fear for trust, and anger for compassion and remorse for forgiveness.

Developing an absolute confidence in God's loving care. When you cannot seem to get a moment's peace, even in the bathroom, remember that God is running the world today, so you can sit back and relax. He has it all under control even in the midst of your chaos.

How do we get that peace? Why do so few Christians ever experience real peace in their lives? Donna Partow, in her Book titled "My Life, A Major Motion Picture" says that Christians tend to live at two extremes. The first being those that drive themselves into physical and emotional exhaustion by trying to please God. They are the ones who are the "church ladies." They are there every time the doors are open. They serve on every committee, teach, and do just about anything to be in God's good graces. The second are those who are content to sneak into heaven by the skin of their teeth. They just come to church when it is convenient. They give, but never serve. However, the middle ground leads to sanity. There is peace somewhere in the middle of those two extremes.[42] If you find yourself one of the "church ladies" then we end up living not by *grace* and *peace* but by *grace* and *rules*. We have become very legalistic in our approach to Christianity. We have more "thou shalt not's" in our vocabulary making it hard for anyone with whom we have a relationship to feel anything but guilt around us.

We must get back to the basics. Don't sweat the small stuff. Really. Let it go. Get over it. You are not Wonder Woman! Remember, she is only a comic book character. She doesn't exist. Set your priorities, and remember with every season of your life those will change. If you think you will never be able to find the time to do those things you desire, the only reason you can't is because you have put those constraints on yourself.

The last area of our life that can become out of balance is our spirit. I believe this is the most important of the three. It is the base the holds to other two in place. Learn to wait on God. Pray. Making prayer a priority isn't easy, if it was we would all be doing more of it. It is a commitment that requires slowing down, and overlooking the distractions that surround you, like, the dishes, the laundry, and the everyday rituals of your life. Prayer should be as easy as talking to your best friend. God already knows what is on your mind and in your heart. You may as well

---

42 Partow, Donna, Soon to be a motion picture: new directions for life's dramas/ Donna Partow.

express those things to Him just the way you feel, because what He really wants from you has nothing to do with your delivery, but everything to do with you desire.

Slow down, when you pray don't let your prayers be like the NASCAR races, or faster than a speeding bullet. If your prayer time is like that then you aren't taking time to learn from, to hear from, or just have fellowship with God. Prayer becomes routine and mundane.

Slow down, when your life is veering out of control. You cannot stop a freight train when it is barreling down the tracks at 100 miles an hour, and there aren't any breaks. It is going to derail, and so will you, if your life is out of balance in the area of your spirit.

Secondly, when all else fails, read the directions. The Bible is God's instruction book for your life. Strong believers spend time with God, in His word, every day. John 15:7 says that "if you abide in Me and My word abides in you, ask whatever you wish, and it shall be done for you"

True balance comes through a relationship with God. He has called us to communicate with him. We need to focus not on our will, but His, just as Christ did in the garden when He prayed, "Not my will but Thine be done." That should be our prayer. We do not align God's will with ours; rather we are to align our will with God's. Hebrews 11:6 tells us, "God rewards those you diligently seek Him" Sometimes we have to lean in close to hear Him. Diligently seeking God is staying the course no matter what obstacles might come your way. Be diligent about it.

He will direct your path. He will lead you where, He wants you to go. Doing what He has called you to do. You have a specific task that God has said, "this is what I want you to do" Some of us have missed that. God looks down and says, "Life could have been so different for you had you listened to Me when I called." It is never too late; no I shouldn't say never, because we have all had missed opportunities. Those are like a greased pig; we try to get our hands on it but it is too slippery and it gets away. In our quest to become like the "virtuous" women, we can ask God for His guidance in directing the paths of our lives. Take care of your body, mind (soul) and spirit. God delights in bringing good things to those who call upon Him. Don't give up!

It's time once again to look at a woman in scripture who is one of God's "Designing Women." Her story is found in the gospel of Luke.

Mary and Joseph rose early. They began to discuss the preparations for their journey to the temple in Jerusalem. The days of her purification were complete. Today was the day that they would present their son, Jesus, for circumcision and according to the Law of Moses.

As Mary bathed her young son, she noticed a pure white dove setting on the windowsill. She had only seen pure white doves in cages. She thought of the many times her father had taken doves to be sacrificed in the temple. Today she believed God had sent this dove to remind her of the promise of sending His son. She was reminded the words the angel of the Lord spoke when he told her that her son would be the only begotten son of God. She held her son close to her chest whispering words of thanksgiving into his ear, "Thank you Father, for this precious gift. I am truly blessed."

It was difficult for Mary to understand how all of this had happened. Yet, she was holding the Promise of God in her arms, just as the angel of the Lord spoken.

Just as Mary was dressing her young son, Joseph walked into the house. She was gently caressing their baby boy, and he heard her singing softly, as she was getting him ready for their journey to the temple. He walked over to where they sat.

Joseph kissed the tiny baby's head, "Lord, how can this be? I know He is not my own, not flesh of my flesh, or bone of my bone, but I promise to love Him as though He were." Looking down at Jesus was indeed looking into the face of a miracle. "We will leave for the temple when you are ready," Joseph said touching Mary's arm. "I will get the donkey from the stable and return in just a few minutes for both of you."_

Just across the city in the temple, Anna was waking up to the sound of birds singing. She sat up, and swung her feet from the cot onto the cold stone floor. Her back was stiff and aching. She was feeling every bit eighty-four years old. Grateful for the years God had given her she whispered a prayer, "Lord, this is the day You have made, I will rejoice and be glad in it, for today You have shown favor on this Your servant". Anna had prayed the same prayer for nearly sixty years.

She moved from her cot to the small table and chairs sitting next to her bed. She would think about the day and what it would hold as she sat there planning her day. Every day was different in some ways, but everyday presented opportunities to fast and pray. Today was no different. She knew that many

159

families with newborn babies would be coming to the Temple today. The sounds of the birds in the courtyard indicated that many turtledoves and pigeons would be sacrificed today.

Anna had helped Simeon with the small children for as long as she could remember. Many of these mothers needed reassurance that everything would go well, especially the young mothers who were bringing their first-born sons for circumcision. Anna smiled as she remembered one young mother who was so distraught. She fainted when Simeon picked the baby up and began to pray over the child. She hoped today would not be such a day. She was ready to bring comfort to those young mothers.

She got up from the chair next to her bed, and rubbed her aching hands. She was much older now. It seemed that with each new day it became increasingly more difficult to do simple tasks; like combing her hair, because her hands were stiff and sore. Nevertheless, today was a special day. Something within her caused her to feel joy that she just could not quite understand.

She had served in the temple ever since the death of her husband. They had only been married seven years before his death. Just as she had done every day for the past sixty years Anna prayed "God of heaven and earth, let this Thy servant see your Glory today. _

Mary sat down after dressing her son and began to nurse him. Once again, she remembered the words the angel had told her, "You shall call his name, Jesus." He was the Messiah, the long awaited Savior.

For months before His birth she prayed, and spent many hours just thinking about what was taking place inside her. She had carried God's Son. He was here, just as it was promised. A smile crossed her face and she whispered into baby Jesus' ear, "Do you know who you are my little one? You will someday." For now Mary and Joseph were to raise their son just as they would have had he been a <u>normal</u> boy. He was normal, in every way, to her. She did not know that one day this child she held would perform miracles, and wonders beyond anything her mind could understand. Jesus closed his eyes, and went to sleep in Mary's arms. All was well in the world for her.

Joseph returned to the room where Mary and Jesus were sitting, and said to her, "Mary, it is time for us to leave, I see our son is quite content, and well fed I'm sure. Maybe he will sleep for a while. I am sure he will not be sleeping in just a little while." Joseph chuckled. Mary turned to him and spoke softly so as not to wake the baby, "Joseph!" was all she said. He knew that she was *not amused by his chuckle. The smile left his face and he spoke again to Mary, "I'm sorry Mary, I know that he will not be happy after the circumcision and I should have been more sensitive to your feelings in the matter----and his." Joseph reached out to Mary and she handed Jesus into the loving arms of his father, his earthly father, and offered a prayer to his heavenly Father. She knew today was going to be hard on all of them so she did not say anything else to him, but took his arm and moved towards the door. They both loved their son. Today was a special day, and nothing was going to spoil it for them. They left Bethlehem and began their journey to Jerusalem._*

After Anna finished praying, she rose from her knees, and walked to the bed. She folded the bedclothes then laid them on the cot. She then took the pitcher of water from the table, and poured it into the basin to wash her face and hands. The water was cool, and felt refreshing on her face. After washing her face, she always felt more awake. Today was no different. She opened the window and poured the water from the basin onto the little bed of flowers beneath her windowsill. They too needed to be refreshed. Just as she emptied the basin, a breeze blew the scent of the roses, and lilacs into the room.

Again, Anna whispered a prayer, "How great are you Lord! You sent the breeze to bring a sweet aroma into this musty old room, just when I need it most. Thank you." Anna felt especially close to the Lord today. Something special was about to happen. Today God was going to give Anna a special blessing._

When Mary and Joseph arrived at the temple, the courtyard was already filled with mothers and fathers of newborn babies. She looked around to see if there was anyone there she knew... It has been several months since Mary has seen anyone from Jerusalem, but she did not recognize anyone. Joseph helped Mary off the donkey as she cradled Jesus in her arms. He then untied the cage that held the turtledoves and pigeons to be sacrificed. Joseph was a carpenter, and buying a lamb was too costly, so today they would bring the doves and the pigeons.

"There are many people here today," Mary spoke to Joseph, "do you see anyone here that we know?"

"No. Surely, we have not been gone so long that we would not recognize old friends. It has only been a few months."

"Of course not, I'm sure it is just that there are so many people here today. Let's make our way to the courtyard, Jesus is beginning to wake up, and I am afraid he will want to be fed before long. I don't want him to start crying before we even receive the blessing."

"Alright," Joseph said as he led them toward the temple courtyard.

Once they arrived, they were greeted by Simeon, the temple priest. Simeon had been praying for many years that God would let him live long enough to see the Lord's Christ. When he took Jesus in his arms be began to praise God saying " Now Lord, you can let thy servant leave this world in peace for today I have witnessed Your salvation which you have prepared in the presence of all people."

Mary and Joseph stood amazed hearing Simeon speak about their son in this manner. How did he know? Simeon blessed them and said to Mary," Behold, this Child is appointed for the fall and rise of many in Israel. Many will oppose Him and a sword will pierce even your own soul. Even through his rejection, many will see the truth as God reveals who they really are.

Anna was standing nearby watching and listening as Simeon spoke to the young parents of Jesus. She moved towards the young couple, and began giving thanks to God. She continued to tell all who would listen that God had sent redemption to Jerusalem in the form of a baby boy named Jesus.

She could not help but laugh and cry all at the same time. For years she had heard Simeon pray and never once had she heard him speak to another mother or father as he had done today. For years she had prayed herself that God would allow her to be a witness to the coming Messiah and today her prayers were answered.

For years Anna had been a faithful servant in the temple. She prayed faithfully to God and worked in the temple day and night for many years. Anna was a young woman when she came to work at the temple and was 84 years old when Mary and Joseph brought Jesus to the temple. She served the Lord faithfully, and given what we know about Anna, I believe that we can credit her with being a woman of righteous character.

Wonder woman exists only in the comic strips but God sees each of you as wonderful women. His desire is that you to become all you can be for His glory. When you learn to balance the three areas of your life, which we have explored in this chapter, you will experience peace and contentment. It is only when we are walking in the spirit of truth we are able to become women by God's design.

If we live as long as Anna wouldn't it be wonderful to know that God was ready and waiting to bless you with something totally unexpected, because you walked with him all the days of your life. You will find time to do all the things your heart desires. When you lay your head down at night you will sleep well, because God will give you the rest you need when you have been faithful to take care of physical, and the spiritual body he has entrusted to you.

Digging Deeper:

1. How do you spend your time? Are you trying to fit too much into your day? Read again Genesis 1:2. At the end of creating what did God do?

   _____.

2. How are you taking care of all three areas of your body, the mind, the soul AND the spirit? List some of those here _____

   _____

3. Are you giving more attention to the physical body than the spiritual body? Yes ___ No ___ Read Deut. 6: 5-9. These verses were known by the Jews as the **Shema** and were God's law for living in total commitment to the Lord.

4. When you diligently seek God what will He do? Read Hebrews 6:11 _____. We all want to be Wonder Woman especially to our family but we have to realize that if any area of our lives is out of balance then everything else will suffer.

Pray and ask the Lord:

Lord you created my mind, my soul and my spirit to work in harmony with one another. Please help me to create balance within my life and show me the areas that are most lacking. Keep me from wasting time on things that will not honor you. Give me peace and help me to create an atmosphere of love and peace within my home. Help me to love my husband and children as you have loved us.

Design #18

"MOTHER KNOWS BEST"

Proverbs 31:28-29– "Her children rise up and bless her;
Her husband also, and he praises her, saying: 29"Many
daughters have done nobly, But you excel them all.

We are going to look at two verses in this chapter because they are part of the same thought. We see two key things in these verses: First, the blessing from her children, and secondly, the admiration of her husband.

If you are a wife and mother reading this, think back to a time when you heard words of admiration from any member of your immediate family. Do you remember a time when your children stood up, and blessed you, or you heard words of admiration from your husband? Most of us would have to think long and hard to come up with anything.

For the most part, we just don't expect it. We don't look for it, nor do we ask for it, but let's face it being a wife and mother can be a pretty thankless job. Or, so it would seem.

I can look back over my childhood, youth and even my young adulthood, and cannot remember a time when I went to my mother and said, "Bless you mom for being a stable person in my life, for providing a Godly example to me. Showing me what it means to be a Christian wife and mother. Why then would I expect my own children to do what I had not done myself?

Here is some of what I have learned. In my own life as a wife, and a mother I can thank my mother for shaping me into the person I am. She exemplifies the virtuous woman herself. I don't think I would be where I am today, no I KNOW I would not be where I am today, had she not been the kind of woman she is. She lives out her faith every day. She prayed for me then and she prays for me now. I did not always see her praying, but I knew she was. We have spoken many times about her prayers for me and for my family.

Whatever I learned about being a good mother, I learned from her. I did not learn it from reading a book. I learned by example. Was I good at it? Sometimes I was, and other times I felt as though I had somehow failed.

My children are grown now, but there is one thing that I am certain about, they know I love them. As with most teenagers, respect was not part of their daily vocabulary, which made those difficult years. Some families I knew had it easy. They had easy children. The progression into the teenager years was as natural for them as breathing is for you and me. No trouble, no worry. Not so, with me. Oh, I wanted it to be easy, but it was not. My daughter was especially challenging during those teen years, and I was not sure that either one of use would live to tell about it. Some of that was my fault, some of it hers. I had never been the parent of a teenage, and I did not have friends who had been parents of teenagers, so we were all going down this road together.

When it came time for my son to be a teenager I strapped on the weapons of warfare, and headed into battle never looking back. I had faced this giant before. This time I was determined to be prepared for it, however I was not. It was during that time that my husband had left the ministry and things in our life began to crumble. It was also during this time, that I had begun to shut down emotionally. I just didn't think I had the strength to face another day. I would do what I had to do to survive, nothing more. The kids were fighting with each other and I was trying to hold the family together by a single thread, even it was unraveling.

My daughter had graduated from high school during this time. She had decided that she wanted to be on her own, and my son just did not want his life disrupted in any way. I did what I could to try to keep the family unit intact. It was like fighting a war with a peashooter. Impossible! Impossible for me, but not for God. I learned to let go and let God work all things together for His purpose.

Through those years I stood firm in my faith. I couldn't always see God's hand, but I knew I could trust His heart. There were days when I was not even sure He was there. I just stood on the truth of His word–He promised to never leave me not forsake me. The words of Moses in Deuteronomy "Be strong and courageous, do not be afraid or tremble at them, for the LORD your God is the one who goes with you. He will not fail you or forsake you." were Gods words that continued to keep me going.

Today, I have no doubt that God has been faithful to me, because the relationship I have with my children is strong and healthy. They know if they ever need anything, or anyone, I am going to be there for them. They will never be able to say that I did not love them unconditionally.

Just this morning as I was praying for them, the picture of my son as a young boy flooded my memory. I remembered him climbing in my lap when he was sick, and hurting. I just rocked him until the pain went away. I hadn't thought about that in years. I loved those moments!

Every day is an opportunity for us to practice being "Christ-like" in front of our children and husbands, in front of our co-workers, family, friends, the clerk in the grocery store, our neighbors. Everyone whose life we touch during the day God gives us opportunities to practice being Proverbs 31 women.

When I first started writing this book I was writing it because I wanted to write a book about something I myself needed to learn. It was a journey of discovery. I know there are many books that have been written on this subject. I thought about what I needed to know, and what I have learned about God's word. How His word applies to my life was the catalyst that began the process.

I must tell you, with each chapter written it has become more and more a book *for* me. You see God's word is relevant for every season of life, for every circumstance of life, for every day of your life. Things that will set you apart from other women and cause your family to take notice, rise up and bless you, are the small things you do that show Christ's love to them and to the worl

I am humbled, really humbled by that fact. We spend so much time gathering roses that we never stop to enjoy them. In my office are several pictures. I have two offices, and they have several pictures in them, a lot of pictures. I am a picture fanatic. I love pictures of places I have been, and the people I love. You won't find pictures painted by other people, or photographs taken by someone else in there. These pictures reflect places I have been, beautiful places. They reflect people I love, beautiful faces of my children and grandchildren. They represent what brings me joy. I <u>love</u> to display pictures of places I have been, and show off my family.

I want to challenge you to do something that may take you out of your comfort zone. When you get up in the morning or today as you finish this chapter, and move through whatever part of your day is left, take time to be intentional about building relationships. Not just those of your immediate family but those within your circle of influence. It could be as simple as a smile or a touch from you. We never know the kind of day someone is having, or how this simple act can change what would have been a horrible day into something they will never forget.

I want to share a story with you. My days are not always happy, and filled with great and wonderful things. I had been having a particularly difficult week (some weeks are like that); it started when I began to work on this chapter. It was a week ago, I sat down for three hours, and I wrote, I had prayed before I began. I thought when I finished the chapter that I had accomplished a great deal. Writing is not always easy. It can be physically and mentally exhausting.

After I completed the chapter I inserted a disc to save it and hit the save button, or so I thought, somehow I had failed to save it. The whole chapter that I had just worked on for three hours was gone. I was upset and frantic trying to find it, but I couldn't. For the next couple of days I was feeling sorry for myself. I just didn't have the heart to try to retype what I knew I could never get back. Thoughts are like words once they are spent you can never get them back.

My week started badly and continued to get worse, but just when you least expect it God shows up. I was having lunch with a friend, and our waiter was a kind young man. He served us with a smile. He wanted to make sure that we were taken care to the best of his abilities. Now that little act of kindness might not seem like much to most people, but to me it was significant. I know that he brightened my day, though he may not know it.

When I needed God to show up in my life, He did. I did not realize it at the time because I was hurting, but not only did he send a smile and kind word through this young man, (who did not even know he was the conduit), but he spoke words of truth and encouragement through His word.

I told you that story for this reason. You are a vessel that God will use so that your family will see you actively showing the love of Christ in tangible ways. A touch, a soft-spoken word, reading to a child. Fixing a meal or playing catch. Whatever it is, they will notice.

My life has always been busy. I always seem to have a million things on my plate. There are times when I need to slow down. My greatest memories are those with my children, rocking them to sleep, or playing some silly game. Making cupcakes with my grandchildren or sitting in the floor playing "Old Maid". When I fix a meal that my husband loves and I know it pleases him, then I am happy. I forget that sometimes. Go back and read the previous chapter if you need a little help with the Wonder Woman syndrome.

At the end of my time here on earth, I want my family to know they were loved by me and by their Heavenly Father more than anyone else in their life was. What do you want your family to know about you? You know we can work so hard at being Wonder Woman that we miss the simple joys of just being a mother, and a wife.

This Sunday will be Mother's Day. On television and the radio there have been many stories told about mothers. This afternoon I heard a ten-year old little girl call our Christian radio station. She was in trying to win a trip for her mother. The radio personality asked her what was special about her mother. She said simple things like, she cooks for me every night. She takes care of my four brothers, sisters, and me. Then the radio personality asked her, "What has your mother taught you." Her answer blew me away. She said, "She has taught me to be truthful and kind and love God." That mother is living this verse.

I know that our lives are busy. So many demands are made for our attention, but you have to be the one to teach them to be truthful, and kind, and to love God. You have to practice those in front of them. You cannot just tell them, you have to show them. If you do, you *will* be blessed among women. Your children *will* rise up and call you blessed. I don't know about you, but I cannot think of anything greater in this world than that. I want my Lord to receive glory for all that I do, and I know that if my children and husband see anything great in me it is because of Him. I cannot take any of the credit. If that is your desire then I believe that you will be blessed. You are well on your way.

I want to try to bring you a glimpse of another woman in scripture. We cannot fully know outside of heaven the impact these women have had on our world. We know quite a lot about this woman. She was a mother like no other. Her name is Mary and she was the mother of Jesus. I am humbled to right about her and a little afraid that I will not do her justice. Mary displayed the attribute of servant-hood. God called her for a purpose, and that purpose was profound. Her life was not always filled with joy. It was also filled with suffering. She was still a mother and as a mother, she wanted the world to know how great her son was (sound familiar).

Here is just one small glimpse into her life and her relationship with her son, Jesus!

The road was hot and dusty as Mary walked along with her family, and friends to Cana.

As Mary walked along the road to Cana, the sandals on her feet were of little comfort. She longed to sit and rest her weary body. She was thankful for the light breeze blowing across her face. The small drops of sweat on her face provided some cool comfort when the breezes blew.

She could hear Jesus' brothers talking about him. She had not seen Jesus since he left home, only a short time ago. My how the years had flown, she thought. As she thought back to his childhood, it was hard for her to believe that her son was the Son of God; Mary could hear her sons talking about times they shared as a family. Her heart was filled with sorrow and joy all at the same time. Not wanting to spoil the fun she kept these things in her heart, as she was accustomed to doing. She would soon see Jesus face to face, and the thought of seeing him again made her smile.

As they walked, Mary could see children playing, and laughing. She remembered Jesus as a young boy sitting in the temple with elders. He was no ordinary child. They had been to Jerusalem and were returning home. Mary and Joseph walked along talking with others making their way home never realizing that Jesus was not with them. Jesus was twelve years old at the time. She remembered how frightened she was when she realized he was not with them. Mary and Joseph searched the entire caravan, but were unable to find him. She was frantic with worry. They had to leave the other children with friends and return to Jerusalem to look for him. They found him in the temple. Jesus seemed to be surprised. She remembered His words to her that day, "Did you not know I would be here, doing my Father's work?" How could they have known, he was just a boy.

Mary wiped the small drops of sweat from her face as she remembered that day. She and Joseph were angry with him, but somehow they could not be angry when he told them he was doing his Father's work. Mary laughed as she remembered Joseph's puzzled look "My Father's business, what has carpentry got to do with teaching in the temple," he whispered to Mary. She touched his arm and told him "I will tell you later, for now let's just get him back home." Joseph knew just exactly what Mary was going to say, "He is God's Son."

Mary knew her son was God's son, but He was her son too, and she could not imagine her life without Him.

When they reached their destination, Mary saw him. Jesus was standing with His disciples talking. He looked different to her, but she dismissed the change. It had to be because she had not seen him in a while. Mary had not heard about the baptism by John, but she had been hearing news that Jesus had begun his ministry, and he was traveling with his disciples. This was what Jesus was born to do. She had no idea of what it would cost Him, or what it would cost her.

Talking with His disciples, Jesus turned and saw his mother. The look in His eyes told them of the great love He had for His mother. Jesus excused himself, and as He approached Mary she ran towards Him, and they embraced. He was not a little boy any longer. He was a man, a man called to greatness.

Mary kissed her son on the cheek and spoke, "My son, my son, how good it is to see you, I have missed you."

Jesus replied, "Mother, I have missed you as well. Come I have some men I want you to meet." He took Mary by the hand and led her towards the group of men gathered near the courtyard. Mary thought as they walked how small her hand seemed in his. She had watched him grow into the man he was, standing beside her, and something in her heart ached. She couldn't quite understand the feeling, for the moment she would put it aside. For now, she would walk with Him to greet His friends.

After the pleasantries and introductions, Mary excused herself. She moved towards the house where the other women were gathered. The wedding feast had been going on for several days when Mary arrived, and she could see that all who were attending were enjoying themselves. Light-hearted music was playing. The bride was still in seclusion waiting to be presented to the groom.

Mary thought back to her own marriage thirty years ago to Joseph. They were young; she had grown to love him more every day. God had blessed their lives together, and she was grateful.

It was customary, in those days, for the guests to help with the cost of such a feast. Mary could see that there seemed to be some concern among the servants, so she approached one of them and asked. "Is there something that I can do?"

"We have run out of wine!" the servant replied "and it will not go well for our master among his guests"

Mary touched the servant's arm and said "Don't worry I will return in a moment." Mary saw Jesus standing in the courtyard and approached him. Leaning up close to his ear, she whispered, "The guests have no more wine."

"Mother, what would you have me do, my hour has not yet come?" Jesus replied, his words tender yet firm. Jesus knew this moment would begin his road to the cross, but Mary only knew that there would be embarrassment for the groom.

Mary knew that Jesus was God's son. She knew He could help with this situation so she motioned for the servants to come to where she and Jesus were standing.

"Do exactly as He tells you." she instructed them.

There were six large water pots nearby. Each pot could hold twenty to thirty gallons each. Jesus instructed the servants to fill each pot with water, as much as each of them would hold and then take the water to the headwaiter.

The servants looked at each other, not knowing what else to do; they did just as Mary had told them. They obeyed Jesus' command.

Mary and Jesus watched, as the headwaiter tasted the water that had now become wine. Mary touched Jesus' arm as she realized what He had done. It was a miracle, the first of many she was sure.

The relationship that Mary had with her son is not well described in the passage in John. What we see though is that even though Mary may not have understood the depth of Jesus' calling she knew who He was. She knew who God was. She had been the recipient of the miracles of God herself, and as God's son, she knew what He was capable of doing. Mary's concern for the guests at the wedding feast prompted her to ask something extraordinary of her son.

How many times have we seen untapped abilities in our children and have encouraged them to move beyond what they wanted, and what was comfortable, to do something that only God knows the far-reaching implications of? We see giftedness in them that no one else can see. As mothers, God has richly blessed us with a sense of discernment when it comes to our children. That is why we are so protective of them. We hurt when they hurt and we rejoice when they rejoice. Sometimes their strongest critics, other times the greatest encouragers.

You are special to your family. They may not say it, but if you love them unconditionally, they will know it. They cannot help but notice, and the day will come when they will take notice of the gift God has given them— you. I love to hear children thanking their mothers for contributing to their successes. You will excel above all other women in their eyes!

Digging Deeper:

1. Read Proverbs 22:6 What is God's promise in this verse?

    _____

2. The word train in Hebrew is *Hanak* and seems in include the idea of setting aside, narrowing or hedging in. Read these verses and see what the result of this type of parenting may bring.

    Proverbs 22:3-4, 9, 11 and 16.

3. In 1 Peter 3:1-4 Wives are to _____ to their husbands (vs. 1) so that they may won by _____ in the way that they _____.

4. What are the imperishable qualities that are valuable to God? (vs. 4)

    _____

Prayer this Prayer:

Dear Father, thank you for Godly wives and mothers. Thank you for bringing (your mother or someone you know) into my life to show me how to be a woman of excellence. Bless her Lord with richest blessings. Give me strength and courage Lord to be all that you have called me to be for my family. To show compassion to a world so that they will see my faith in You. Amen.

Design #19

"ALL IN FAVOR, SAY CHRIST"

Proverbs 31:30- Charm is deceitful and beauty is vain, but a woman who fears the Lord, she shall be praised[43]

The first word in this verse brings many different definitions with it. Here is Webster's definition of the word charm;

1 a: the chanting or reciting of a magic spell: INCANTATION
   b: a practice or expression believed to have magic power

2: something worn about the person to ward off evil or ensure good fortune: AMULET

3 a: a trait that fascinates, allures, or delights
   b: a physical grace or attraction — used in plural
   c: compelling attractiveness

4: a small ornament worn on a bracelet or chain

5: a quantum characteristic of subatomic particles that accounts for the unexpectedly long lifetime of the J/psi particle, explains difficulties in the theory of the weak force, is conserved in interactions involving electromagnetism or the strong force, and has a value of zero for most known particles[44]

43
44 Merriam-Webster, Inc: *Merriam-Webster's Collegiate Dictionary*. 10th ed. Spring-

I can fully grasp all concepts, except for number five, so please forgive my ignorance if you can understand that charm is a quantum characteristic of a subatomic particle!

The word charm here is the word **chen** in the Hebrew– the word means favor. Here the writer of Proverbs says favor is deceitful and beauty is vain. Let's once again try to unpack all that verse has to offer us.

Cinderella, Sleeping Beauty, Snow White, Barbie, what do all of these fictional characters have in common? Beauty, innocents, purity. However, they are not real. So why do all little girls want to dress up and pretend they are one of them?

There is no problem with pretending, but what happens when we grow up and the world does not see us as those "little princesses" any longer? What happens when we reach the awkward age of ten or twelve or maybe even fifteen or sixteen and we aren't cute anymore. If the world places all of its value on the external, we can certainly understand why so many young women devalue themselves, or have been devalued by the society.

The first part of this verse really isn't about physical beauty at all or the compelling attractiveness of this woman. Although, I believe she was a beautiful woman because the author deals with that in the second part of the verse. But, "favor is deceitful" puts a different spin on what we would think of here.

The same word used here in our passage (*chen*) is the same word used to describe Noah's relationship with the Lord in Genesis 6:8. The word or some form of the word is used over 100 times in scriptures in various contexts. The truth is that we all want to find favor in someone's eyes. Did that sink in? We ALL want to find favor in someone's eyes. Where you find favor is important. Abraham, Noah and Hannah and many others in scripture sought to find favor from the Lord, not from man.

Since we know that Satan is a liar, and a deceiver, we ought to beware of his schemes to draw us away from finding favor in Christ, and into finding favor with man. God gave us these desires, but He wants us to get all we need *from* Him, and find all we need *in* Him.

Let me be very transparent for a moment here and tell you my story. As an only daughter, I know that my father and mother see me very differently than I see myself. My father has always called me his "baby girl." I know that my parents see me very differently than the rest of the world. I am their daughter and nothing can change their love for me. I have found favor in their eyes. I have sought to bring honor to them, to please them in my words, and actions. I know they are proud of the woman that I am. I have not always brought them great pleasure. (I was once a teenager with a mind of my own.) I did however grow up, not only physically, but also emotionally. However, finding favor with God has not always been top priority in my life.

There was a time in my life that finding favor from others was very important so much so that it consumed me. I wanted desperately to be liked and even loved and it broke my heart to be rejected.

In my senior year of high school, I had a friend. She and I spent almost all of our spare time with each other. We lived in the same neighborhood, went to the same school, and even the same church. We were the two-peas-in-a-pod, so to speak. When you saw one of us, the other was somewhere close by. We shared our most intimate secrets with each other. She was a talented pianist and I was a singer. We were in the youth choir together and enjoyed many of the same things. It was a relationship that I valued, a little too much, because one day I received a phone call and she was on the other end of the phone telling me that she no longer wanted to be my friend. I was devastated. I could not understand. It didn't make sense we were best friends. It took the wind right out of my sail. I withdrew and asked "Why me, what had I done?" I had lost friends before which hurt but this, this was cruel and I couldn't get over it.

For years I prayed for a friend to come along and fill that hole in my heart that she had left. I moved a lot and every place I lived I tried to develop some lasting friendship, one that I was sure would stand the test of time. I wanted the kind of friendship I had only heard about. The kind of friendship where girlfriends would get together, share stories, laugh and cry. One that, even though they were miles apart they could call one another talk as though they had never been apart. I have wonderful friends in my life now, but that has not always been true for me.

God had to show me, through those painful relationships, that I needed to place a higher priority on my relationship with Him. More than any earthly relationship. He wants to be our best friend. The one who fills our hearts with joy and laughter. The one who sees us as we are and still longs to be with us. He wants us to desire His favor, not that of man.

For the many years after losing friendship with my best friend I sought to find favor through my singing. I sang in church and in my community every opportunity I had. Then we moved to Texas! God put my prideful heart on the shelf. No longer was I going to be in the spotlight. God had to get my attention some way to save me from my own self-destruction.

What I lost in my relationship with my friend I was trying to make up for, by getting my "strokes" emotionally from my singing. I was singing for the Lord so I thought it was okay to have the praises of people. However, when I was filled with my own pride God said. "Okay, young lady, you need to sit this one out." For two years I sang in the choir, but I never had a solo part, I was never asked to sing for any program, nothing.

It was painful, but necessary. In that two-year period God began to change my heart. I said, " Okay Lord if I never sing again I will find some other area of ministry." After this two-year sabbatical, I was once again asked to sing. I was so scared, afraid that I would dishonor God and that I would fall into pride again that I didn't want people to say anything nice about me, ever!

Again, that was not enough. I still didn't get it. I thought I was humble, that I had learned my lesson, that I was okay with God. Not so. Years go by and my heart still needs transformation. Fast forward. God gave me a verse of scripture shortly afterwards that I have found key to my life. Philippians 1:6. He (meaning Christ) who has begun a work in me (Pam) will continue to perfect me right up until the day He calls me home. (My paraphrase). Finding favor with anyone other than God will leave you empty and unfulfilled. When we seek to please Him above everything else in this world we will be satisfied. While I was trying to find happiness outside of Christ, He was, and is continuing to work on the inside. I cannot change the circumstances of my life, but I can choose the one I will trust with my life.

The second part of this verse is important as well. Beauty is vain. I couldn't agree more. By the time we reach the ripe old age, whatever that is, beauty may have long since been a thing of the past. Like so many young women today I too, have struggled with the idea of beauty. It is all around us. On television, in magazines, on billboards, in the movies. Everywhere you go someone it trying to sell beauty. You cannot look up anything on the internet without seeing ads for beauty products, weight loss, teeth whitening, or hair styling. All trying to make us into the beauty queens we dream of becoming.

Once again, this is another of Satan's lies. We buy it though. The beauty industry reaps great benefits from our need to be beautiful. On average worldwide, we spend about forty-five to sixty billion dollars on cosmetics, hair styling, waxing, tanning, curling, straightening, nipping and tucking, starving and exercising our way to perfection. No matter how much we work on looking beautiful we cannot stop the process of aging. Yuck! I hate it. Every morning I go through this ritual of shampooing and styling my hair, painting my face and layering cosmetics over moisturizer and wrinkle fillers. Does anyone care that it takes me forty-five minutes to an hour e-v-e-r-y single day, 365 days a year without exception, to get ready. I am afraid someone will come to the door and see me without makeup, (which is a scary thought, even to me!) so even when I don't plan to go anywhere I go through this ordeal. I am so used to it that it is no big deal, until I have a bad hair day, or I haven't slept, and there are dark circles under my eyes, or I slept too long on one side and my face has a crease in it that no amount of makeup can cover. Then I might be paranoid. Again, does anyone really care?

Earlier in the book, I talked about the importance of taking pride in your appearance and I still maintain that we should, but here is what I think we need to understand. God is, and always will be, far more concerned with who we are inside than what we look like on the outside. For some of us this is so hard to deal with because we do not feel pretty, and it is work to look good. When we have a bad hair day, we are ready for a meltdown.

I was walking through the halls at work last week and several women I know were coming in and out of the office. Some of them were not particularly stunning women, some were dressed in t-shirts and blue jeans, looking somewhat ordinary, and you know what I never gave it a thought. I did not stop to think, "She sure looks plain or why doesn't she wear makeup and fix her hair a little differently." I saw those women the way I believe God does. They are wonderful, compassionate, caring, spectacular, gifted women, all who are loved passionately by God. Really. I thought, "Do you think people really are worried about the fact that your hair is flat today or your makeup isn't perfect?" No and if they are then something is wrong with them not with you." Beauty will fade away. We will become old someday and what do you really want people to know and think about you when your beauty is gone?

The last part of this verse really is the heart of the verse. ***But, a woman who fears the Lord, she shall be praised.*** Now that is my prayer for you and for me. A woman who fears or has reverence for the Lord is a woman who shall be praised. If you spend all your efforts on the physical beauty and neglect your inner beauty you have wasted all your efforts on the temporal things of this world. When you reach the end of your life will you be able to stand before the Lord a woman worthy of praise?

I am talking to every one of us who will read these words, myself included. I can work every day to look beautiful, but if I don't spend any time at all on my relationship with the One who created me, and gave me life, the one who loves me even without makeup, then it is all in vain.

There is a great lesson for us as we come to the end of our journey together toward becoming women by God's design. How can we not be changed? If your heart's desire and mine is to be a woman who longs to be like this magnificent woman of Proverbs 31 then let's do that. Let's take the next step. Let's run towards Him, Christ, who is running towards you with open arms. Running to catch you when you fall, running to hold you when you weep, running to save you from harm, to lift up your head when despair threatens or over take you.

Angela Thomas in her book "When Wallflowers Dance" urges women to live lives with righteous confidence. The confidence that keeps us from becoming obscure and unnoticed. The life that pushes us away from the wall into the arms of our heavenly father who wants us to dance. Oh, I have to admit that I want to live that life but sometimes I tell God, "couldn't I just blend in, being a wallflower really isn't so bad. It's safe against the wall. No one sees me and if no one sees me then I won't get hurt. Life hurts and couldn't I just become an unwoman." God let me say those words to him not long ago and then he asked me a question. "Do you really want to be a wallflower, really? I can let you stay against the wall, if that is really what you want, but if you do then we won't be able to dance. You have to step away from the wall, take my hand, close your eyes and let me guide you across the dance floor of life. It is going to uncomfortable for you at first but I am a great teacher so don't worry before long you will be dancing like you have been dancing your whole life." I get it. Abandonment. Letting go. I wrote a study a year ago for a conference session that I was leading on what I call the 7 Stages of Healing and the word healing is an acronym each letter representing a different stage in our healing process and the letter L represents letting go. Letting go of past hurts and failures and holding onto God's hand and letting Him walk, run and dance you through your journey on this earth.

It's hard, no doubt, life is hard. We are going to face trials and disappointments, hurts that we think will never go away. When my friend told me that she did not want to be my friend I never really got over that. I carried that hurt with me. I didn't know just how much I had let those words impact the person I would become. It seems like such a little thing, you just move on, it was teenage cruelty, but I had already felt like a wallflower. I wasn't at all beautiful, I wasn't athletic, I wasn't popular, I just was. So to be told you are not worthy to be my friend was like telling me you have no value. I was determined to never feel that way again. I carried that pain around with me for years, and years, and even more years. As I write these words, I realize it still hurts. I really did just want someone to ask me to dance. Not literally although I love dancing. I just wanted to be loved for being me, and God **does**.

The reverence we have for God comes from a right relationship with Him. To really *know* Him. Are you ready to know God? I am. I stand in awe of Him. I am amazed by His love. I can't fully understand it. I can't fully get my mind around it, I know who He is, but I want to really know WHO He is. He is the Almighty God. Creator of the universe. The One who breathes life into every living thing. The One who sees and knows all there is to know. Yet came to earth in the form of a man to die an unbelievable death of shame and agony, nailed to a cross for me, for you. Christ suffered far more than I will ever suffer. Yes He is God, He can handle it, but His spirit lives within us, and He has equipped us to handle it with His help. He knows our weaknesses, and He is our shield, and our deliverer. There is nothing that we cannot face together. Nothing.

How can we be a wallflower when He has called us to a life of so much more? If we believe in our hearts what we have seen and heard about God we will have to dance. We won't be able to stand back against the wall. Do you feel it, your foot, is it tapping? You know you want to dance, so get out there and dance.

Here is another amazing woman her name is Mary Magdalene, from the book of John.

The sun was coming up soon, Mary Magdalene thought as she wiped away the tears she had been shedding all night, "I have to get to the tomb, I have to see Him." Her mind flashed back to the evening of His death. The pain of Jesus' death fell on her heart like a heavy rock. So much so that she found it hard to breath. Did it really happen? Was He really gone? It had been three days but Mary didn't remember any of them. She hadn't eaten or slept much since that day.

Mary's thoughts were immediately taken back to the moment she met Him. He had saved her life; at least he saved her from a life of unbelievable suffering. Jesus had delivered her from seven demons. She remembered the day as clearly now as she did then. The sun was rising, just as it was on this morning, when He came to her. She wasn't in her right mind. People were afraid of her. They called her crazy. They didn't want to have anything to do with her. Yet this man, Jesus, touched her and called the demons out of her, and she was free. She let her mind go back to that day because even though He was gone from her she knew that because of Him, she would never be the same.

That day Mary of Magdala was set free. Mary was a follower of Christ. When she learned of his arrest she ran to the home of Jesus' mother, Mary, to be with her. The days that followed his arrest were agonizing. Mary stayed with Jesus' mother and she was with her when they crucified Him.

Another wave of tears flooded her eyes, and she wept uncontrollably, falling to the floor as she pictured His body hanging there on the cross. He didn't even look the same. His body was beaten beyond recognition. How could anyone be so cruel? Her mind was given to hatred for those responsible for His death. Then she remembered the words she had heard Jesus preach to the multitudes of loving your enemies. "I can't do that." she thought, "I can't love the people who took You away from us. I just can't", she whispered through her tears as her fist pounded the floor.

Once again her thoughts were taken back to the moment He had set her free. She was a broken mess that day. Before He set her free she had been given to fits of rage, but since that day she had not felt rage, until now. Everything in her wanted to scream, but something kept her from it. She couldn't explain it, but she remembered what He had said during the last supper before he died. Peter, James and John were with him. He told them they would see him again.

She heard him tell the thief on the cross he would be with Him in paradise. She knew this was not the end.

A strong urgency to get to the tomb overcame her. She quickly rose from the floor and wiped the tears from her eyes. She grabbed her shawl and covered her head as she headed out the door. It was still dark outside, but the sun was beginning to peek through the horizon.

Mary the Mother of Jesus and Salome were also getting ready to go to the tomb to properly prepare Jesus' body for burial. Mary Magdalene hurried to meet Mary and Salome. The three of them walked together to the tomb where Jesus' body was laid.

They talked with each other, consoling one another the best they could. "How will we be able to do this", Salome asked Mary, the mother of Jesus. "He is my son, God will make a way" was all Mary could say. They walked in silence the rest of the way. Mary spoke first as they walked along the road, "Who will roll away the stone from the entrance for us? It is much too heavy; we will have to get some help." Mary Magdalene looked around to see if she could see anyone walking in their direction. She would stop them and ask for their assistance, but she saw no one.

As they approached the tomb the sun was rising. They could see that the stone that had covered the entrance to the tomb was no longer there. Seeing this Mary Magdalene touched Mary's arm. The three of them paused and walked slowly towards the tomb. As they made their way to the entrance they walked cautiously inside the tomb, expecting to find Jesus' body. Instead they saw a man dressed in a white robe sitting at the right of the stone slab that had once held the body of Jesus. His burial clothes were there, but His body was gone.

"Do not be amazed, the man, Jesus of Nazareth, who was crucified, is not here. He is risen. Look, this is the place where he was laid. See this is the cloth that covered His body. He is no longer here. Go and tell the other's that Christ the Lord is risen. Tell Peter and the other disciples that He has gone before them to Galilee and He will meet them there."

They fled the tomb, fear and astonishment gripped them, and they were trembling. They were so frightened that they could not speak to anyone about what they had just witnessed. Mary Magdalene rushed on ahead of them seeking to find anyone who could tell her what had been done with the body of Jesus. The reality that he had truly risen had not sunk in. They believed that someone had stolen his body and Mary was determined to find out who.

Ahead of her on the path, leading away from the tomb where Jesus' body had been placed, she saw a man walking. His head was covered, and she could not see who it was. It didn't matter; she would ask him if he had seen the men who had taken the Lord away. She ran up to him and placed her hand on his arm and spoke, "Please sir, can you tell me where they have taken the Lord?" Mary still had not recognized the man. It was Jesus. When he turned around to her he spoke. "Touch me not, Mary, for I have not yet ascended to My Father in heaven." Mary immediately knew that it was Jesus, and she fell before Him weeping and crying out, "You are alive!"

"Mary, you must tell the others that I have risen just as I said I would. Tell them that I will meet them in Galilee"

Mary wanted to touch him again just to make sure that He was indeed really there. She rubbed her eyes, and under her breath she said "I must be seeing things." It really was Him she knew His voice but, He looked different to her. He did not bare the marks of the man she had seen beaten just a few days before. She could see that He was real, she had touched Him. He was very much alive.

Mary did as Jesus had instructed her. She found the disciples along with Mary, the mother of Jesus, and told them that she had seen Jesus. He had indeed risen from the dead! They thought that in her grief she had lost her mind. It was impossible. Mary reminded them that He had told them He would be raised from the dead. They were not convinced but they would go and see for themselves if what she had told them was true.

Mary could not contain the joy she felt and ran through the street shouting, "He is risen, Jesus Christ the Lord is risen!"

Can you imagine the shock and surprise of Mary when she saw Jesus for the first time after His resurrection? I would imagine that nothing was going to prevent her from proclaiming the good news of Christ. She had seen Him. She had been with Him. She had touched Him. He was alive.

That same joy that Mary had we can have. When He saved us He gave us a reason to proclaim the good news. Christ the Lord is risen, He sits on the throne of heaven at the right hand of His father, and He **will** return one day to call His children home. I am one of those children, are you? If so, praise God, you too can proclaim to good news of Christ. If not, won't you ask Him into your heart right now? When you do you will be among the ones whom God will say, well done good and faithful servant.

DIGGING DEEPER:

1. Do you know God, really know him? Look up these passages to see what the word has to say about God and list what these verses say about who God is. Genesis 1:1, Genesis 14:22, Numbers 24:16, Deut. 5:9, Genesis 21:33, Genesis 22:8, Jeremiah 33:16. Ex 17:15 _____

   _____

   _____

   _____

2. What does this verse Proverbs 1:7 say about the fear of the Lord?

   _____

   _____

3. Read 1 Peter 3:3-4. What does Peter says we should be adorning ourselves with? _____

   _____

PRAY THIS PRAYER:

Father God it is my desire to know You, to know who I am in You. Thank you for Your word. It is the life and light for my life. Thank you that though my life is filled with sin You still beacon me into Your presence. Help me to see myself as You see me. To find my worth in You. Guard my heart and my mind and create in me a clean heart so that others may see Your good work and Glory You. Amen

Design # 20
"The Finished Product"

**Proverbs 31:31- Give her the products of her hands
and let her works praise her in the gates.**

As we approach the end of this book, I hope that you have found within its pages some useful tools in helping you become all the God has designed you to become. My prayer for you will be that God uses you to accomplish His will and expand His Kingdom.

This book has been quite a journey for me. One that has taken quite a long time. I started this not really sure why I needed to even write such a book. So many other men and women have written books on Proverbs so why this one, why me, why now? I think this last verse will answer that question. If God has a plan for your life and mine then for this reason alone His has called you.

Hard work was no stranger to women in the biblical days. I think of the pioneer women who worked harder than most men today. So giving her some sort of accolades for her labor seems quite appropriate to me. What does this verse say about us?

Give her the products or the fruit of her hands. In scripture, the word fruit is used often to refer to what we produce in our lives. We are producing either good fruit or bad fruit. Jesus is the vine, and we are the branches and he that abides in Him bears much *fruit* and apart from Him, we can do nothing. That verse is found in John 15:5 and verse 8 in this same chapter says that God is glorified if we bear much fruit.

Matthew Henry in his commentary on the whole bible says this about verse 31.

"Some are praised above what is their due, but those that praise her do but *give her of the fruit of her hands;* they give her that which she has dearly earned and which is justly due to her; she is wronged if she have it not. Note, those ought to be praised, the fruit of whose hands is praise-worthy. The tree is known by its fruits, and therefore, if the fruit be good, the tree must have our good word. If her children be dutiful and respectful to her, and conduct themselves as they ought, they then *give her the fruit of her hands;* she reaps the benefit of all the care she has taken of them, and thinks herself well paid.[45]

What is the fruit of our labor? That can be many things. As suggested by Matthew Henry here the fruit of our labor can be our children. If we work hard to instill in them the truth of God's word He tells us that His word will not return void. If we train up our children in the way they should go they will not depart from it. They may however, not be walking in the truth of God's word. If we are to receive a reward for our labor then I trust God will bring home the prodigal child. We must never give up on them. Prayer is a powerful tool in the hands of Christians. We cannot under estimate its power to transform lives or to redeem that which was lost. All of our children's lives there can, and will be teachable moments. Moments that God uses to bring truth to them.

We only have one opportunity to make a difference in the lives of those that God has entrusted to us. So go make a difference. If you are a young mother, you can begin to shape the minds of your children towards the things of Christ, right now. You must disciple them, use all those teachable moments in their lives to point them to Christ.

The path that we follow will not be easy. Life is not easy. Oh, I know, you've heard that before, so why do we need to hear it again? Maybe like me, you need a reminder of the mercy and grace of God upon the lives of those who have been faithful. If we labor for the Lord **all** the days of our lives then the reward will be praise in the gates of heaven.

Some time ago, I thought how nice it would be to receive some words of praise from others. You know, someone praising your work, your family

---

45   Henry, Matthew: *Matthew Henry's Commentary on the Whole Bible: Complete and Unabridged in One Volume.* Peabody : Hendrickson, 1996, c1991

thanking you for all you do for them, a pat on the back for a job well done. However, in looking back at that particular moment in my life having the praises of my family, though nice, could not compare to having God's approval of my life. When I needed grace He gave it, when I needed mercy He provided that too. All our lives we should be learning about God's grace and mercy. This is who He IS, and it is that mercy that saved me. The mercy that spared my life, for **His** glory for **His** good pleasure, not so I could feel good about myself. We were created in the image of the Most High God and as we walk this earth we should do so with great humility, for we can do no less, for Him who has done so much for us. We must stand firm in our resolve to be a beacon of hope to a lost and dying world.

Our prayers should be for God to make us into the image of His son, daily laying down our own needs for the needs of others. That is what Proverbs 31 is about. The unselfish giving of ourselves so that ultimately our lives point others to our Father in Heaven. Knowing the Holiness of God should be our desire. It is His mercy, that makes us whole.

Life may not be all we envisioned it to be, but when we choose to walk in the path of righteousness, **oh my sisters**, it will be better than we imagined it would be! Even the dark days of despair will give way to God's glorious light. God wastes not our pain. God moves us from the dark into the light, and brings healing to our wounded soul. We bear His mark on our lives, and when we walk in the way of truth, all of heaven is praising us. The angels will marvel at how in the midst of adversity you found joy unspeakable. Our hope remains steadfast through those days of uncertainty when we follow Him. He will lead you through the storms, and set your feet on solid ground.

God is our refuge and strength, a very present help in time of trouble. We will not fear, though the earth be changed, though the mountains slip into the sea, He will not leave you alone. He will be in your midst. That is a promise found in Psalm 46.

It is that promise that we can stand on. She is a woman of great resolve day after day she remains steadfast in her commitment to God, to love her family and to work without regret, tirelessly for their good. She is an amazing woman. She is you. You are amazing. You're desire to become a woman by God's design is just what God desires for you. What joy you bring to Him who loves you. What a delight you are to Him. The bride of heaven is speaking to the Father saying, "Look at her, isn't she something".

During my separation I continued to serve in my church as an accompanist and one day during a confrontation with my ex-husband he said these words to me, "You must think you are really something special". Those words stung my heart and brought deep agony and hurt as I thought, "no I don't, I'm no one, I don't have any value. You took that away from me" I shared the encounter with one of my pastors. When I told him what he had said his response was, "Well, I hope you said, as a matter of fact I am something special, I am something special to God!" It took me a long time to believe that-- a <u>very long</u> time. I wasted a lot of time feeling sorry for myself. I could not see anything good in me, but I tried really hard to find my worth in everything outside of my worth to God. It wasn't until I realized that God loved me, really loved me, not my talent, not my appearance, that I began to believe that I was special to God. God is the lifter of our heads. When we fall down He takes our chin in His hand, and raises our head up and says to us, "Don't you look down, you keep your head up, and your eyes on me, I am NOT going to let you fall again. Now stand up, and take my hand. We will walk this road together."

Do you remember watching or reading about the 1992 Olympics? There was a young man named Derek Redmond who was preparing to run? Many there that day thought he would take home a gold medal. During the race, something snapped and he fell to the ground in extreme pain. Through his pain, he was determined to finish the race, but every step was shear agony. Watching in the stands was his father. Seeing his son's pain moved him into action, and nothing was going to keep him away from his son. He jumped the rail and ran onto the track next to his son. With his arm around him, he helped him to the finish line. He told him, "We will finish this together." The crowd in the stands stood and applauded. They shouted as the young man hobbled across the finish line.

God is just like that with us. When we cannot finish the race because we are too badly bruised and beaten, He runs past the ones who want to see us fail. He holds us up and says to us, "Come on baby girl, we will finish this together! I am going to help you. You are not alone."

All of heaven applauds and shouts of praise erupt as you cross the finish line. Now, go out and become a woman of great price, a woman worthy of all God has waiting for you, not for your glory, but for His. One day you will lay your crown at his feet and it will have been worth it all.

Let me leave you with one more glimpse into the life of another woman in the Bible. She is the Samaritan woman found in the book of John, chapter 4.

Jesus and His disciples had traveled all day, when they came to the city of Samaria, near the land that Jacob had given his son Joseph. Jacob's well was there and Jesus being tired stopped to rest.

The disciples were talking among themselves, and decided that they should go into town to find food. While Jesus was resting a woman approached the well carrying an empty clay jar.

"Would you give me a drink?" Jesus spoke.

The woman was startled by his request and set down the jar. "Why are you speaking to me, you are and Jew and I am a Samaritan," she asked him? Samaria had long been considered by the Jews a city of idolatry. Jews would have nothing to do with the people of Samaria. The thought occurred to her as she considered his request. What was he even doing in Samaria? Most Jews would walk miles around the city to avoid having to travel through Samaria.

Jesus being very aware of her reluctance to speak to him said, "If you knew the gift of God and who it is that is asking for drink of water you would ask for much more and He would have given you living water"

"Living water, what is this living water and where do you get it," she thought. Then she asked him, "Since you have no pot to draw water in and this well is deep, where can you get this living water? This well was made by Jacob. His sons and all their cattle drank from this well. You are surely are not greater than he is, are you? So how is it possible to have this living water?"

Jesus having great compassion for her spoke again, "Everyone who gets water from this well to drink will have their thirst satisfied but only for a short time. If anyone drinks of the well of living water they will never be thirsty again. The water that I give will become in him a well of water springing up to eternal life."

"I would like to have this water that you speak of, this jar is heavy. If I have

this water that you speak of I will not be thirsty, and I will not have to come here daily to get water." she said and she lifted the jar from the ground.

Jesus knew that she did not understand the water he spoke of so he told her to, "Go and call your husband to come back here to the well with you."

Looking surprised she spoke to him again. This time there was a strange feeling in the pit of her stomach and she replied "Sir, I have no husband."

"I know, you have told the truth, for you have had five husbands and the man that you live with now is not your husband."

"Are you a prophet? How is it that you know this about me? Our fathers worshiped on this mountain, but the Jews say that we must worship in Jerusalem. Is that right?

"This you need to know, there is going to come a day very soon where Samaritans will neither worship here in this mountain, nor in Jerusalem. The Samaritans worship in the dark and the Jews worship in the day. You worship what you don't know anything about, and the Jews worship what they know. Salvation is from the Jews. But, the truth is, right now it doesn't matter who you are, Samaritan or Jew. What matters is that you worship the True God in spirit and in truth. God is looking for those who have this kind of heart. A heart that desires to worship Him. God is spirit and He is seeking those who will worship in spirit and in truth." Jesus said.

"That all sounds good but we are waiting for the Messiah and when he comes He will tell us what we need to do."

Looking into her eyes Jesus said "I am He".

Just then the disciples returned and saw Jesus speaking to the woman. They began to urge him to get some food to eat. This amazed the woman. She was sure that they too would be trying to avoid her, but they said nothing. She left her jar at the well and returned to the village. Once she arrived something happened to her. She knew that the man she had been speaking had to be the Messiah. How else would he know so much about her? She had never seen him before. No one else but Christ could possibly know what he knew.

"Hey everyone, come to the well and meet this man, he told me everything I had ever done. Is it possible that he could be the Messiah?" In her heart, she knew He had to be the Messiah, but she was sure that if they did not come, and see for themselves they would never believe her. They would think she was crazy.

Convinced she had met someone, but certainly not the Messiah, the people of the village decided to see for themselves.

Leading the way, the Samaritan woman in her excitement told them that this man told her all the things she had ever done. He knew about her five husbands, and that the man she no lived with was not her husband.

In the meantime, the disciples were trying to get Jesus to eat something "I have food that you know nothing about," he said, referring to the bread of life. The disciples wondered who had given him food, and each one asked the other "Did you already give him something to eat?" While they stood around trying to figure out who had fed Jesus the woman from Samaria had returned this time she had the whole town with her.

Jesus spoke again asking the disciples to look around. "In just a few months it will be harvest time, take a good look around, I am telling you that right in front of you is a field that is ready to be harvested, the Samaritan people are ready. Let's bring in the harvest"

The woman of Samaria brought all those from town with her to hear this man speak. When he had finished everyone there knew that He was indeed the one they had been hearing about all their lives. He was the Messiah, the long awaited one.

Jesus knew her, had he not spoken to her she would never have known the love of God. The people would not have known. But he spoke with love and compassion, and she knew only God would have done that.

When they returned to the village they begged Jesus to stay with them for a few days, no one had ever cared so much for them. They would have missed it all had it not been for the story of a man named Jesus and the woman at the well.

What a beautiful story of redemption. I think most of us can relate to her story in some way. We may have been going about our daily lives when Jesus showed up. We had no idea that He was going to call us to Him that day. When it happens, just like the Samaritan woman, we run with excitement to tell our family and friends the good news of what God has done in our lives.

I would love to finish the story of this woman. What happened to her after that day at the well? I imagine things were very different for her. Did people see a change in her life? Not everyone that day believed. Was her life a testimony to the grace and mercy of God? As we close out our study of Proverbs 31 I believe this last verse is a direct reflection of a life changed by the power of the Holy Spirit. These verses are not merely verses of some fairytale princess they are verses with real applications for our lives today.

They are just as relevant to us right now, this moment, as they were when they were written. I believe it or I would not have spent this much time writing about it. I have been praying for you; know you are loved by the King of Kings.

Digging Deeper

1. Read Psalm 1. What are some of the benefits of one who delights in the Lord? _____

   _____

   _____

2. Now, read it again and list what happens when we walk in the counsel of the ungodly. _____

   _____

   _____

3. Read Galatians 5:22 and list the fruits of the spirit mentioned in this passage. _____

   _____

   _____

4. In Paul's letter to the Colossians he wrote about their faith and spiritual growth. Read vss. 1-14 and list some of the things that Paul was praying for them. _____

   _____

   _____

   _____

LET'S PRAY TOGETHER ONE MORE TIME:

Father God in heaven, this journey has been long but it has been worth it. When I think I cannot make it you come along side me, lift me up and help me to finish the race. Thank You that You met me at the well and saw in me what I refused to see in myself. You showed me the areas of my life that I had been holding on to and you gave to me living water. I am ready to shine! I am ready to be used for Your glory. I AM a woman by God's design. Amen.

"END"

CPSIA information can be obtained at www.ICGtesting.com
Printed in the USA
LVOW110455291011

252577LV00002B/1/P